# Running to Win!

# Running to Win!
## A Positive Biblical Approach
## to Rewards and Inheritance

---

### G. Harry Leafe

---

**Scriptel Publishers**
Houston, Texas

Copyright © 1992 by
G. Harry Leafe

Published by
Scriptel Publishers
P. O. Box 691046
Houston, Texas 77269-1046

Library of Congress Cataloging-in-Publication Data

Leafe, G. Harry 1940 -
  Running to Win!

    108 p.  cm.
    ISBN 0-9635128-0-3
    1. Sanctification. 2. Faith. 3. Salvation.
  I. Title. II. Title: A Positive Biblical Approach to Rewards and inheritance.
  234

*Printed in the United States of America*

# Acknowledgment

I am very much indebted to Dwight Small for his encouragement and faithful assistance in editing this manuscript. His contribution to this project has greatly impacted my life.

To the memory of Bill Knight and Jay Linebaugh -- two faithful servants of God who loved me and introduced me to life in Christ.

# Contents

# Foreword

"Thy kingdom come!" How many trillions of times has that prayer been made by the children of the Father, but it has probably never been prayed even once with full realization of what He has in store in the kingdom for those who endure the pain and follow faithfully to the end of the race. The grand climax of earth's entire history -- the age to come -- is yet to come. The millennial kingdom -- the victory celebration -- is going to be shared with that portion of the resurrected/raptured Body of Christ that has paid the price of diligent discipleship.

God has a very definite purpose for the period of time between our justification and our glorification which we call "the race." During the in-between, we are becoming by what we do with what He gave us, what we will be in the climactic kingdom age to come. Today is a day of becoming. Then will be a day of being what we have become. There is a continuity -- not a discontinuity --

between how we end the race in this life and how we will reign with Christ (Romans 8:17; 2 Timothy 2:12) in the kingdom climax.

Not until we appear at the Bema (2 Corinthians 5:10) will we receive the final score of the faithful and infallible Judge (1 Corinthians 4:5). And this is a Judge that is really for us. He wants us to receive a "full reward" (2 John v. 8). But He cannot reward that which has not been earned. This is not a gift. It comes from a life of faithful stewardship of our time, talents, and treasure. But the returns from our investment are unparalleled by anything we have seen, heard or imagined.

Dr. Harry Leafe has done for us all an excellent job of not only exercising careful exegetical skill and theological soundness in Scripture, but he has done it with a positive thrust that creates an appetite to dig into the Scripture and examine this tremendous motivational force that, unfortunately, lies dormant in the thought processes of most Christians -- even pastors. See you at the Bema -- if not before -- for no one will be absent.

Earl D. Radmacher, Th.D.
Western Seminary Phoenix
Scottsdale, Arizona

# Preface

Through tear-filled eyes she addressed the question to me: "Pastor, how much is enough?"

That question came as I talked with a lady in our church about recent events in her life. Three years earlier she had lost a seventeen year old daughter in a boating accident. Now she had learned that her only surviving child, a beautiful girl of sixteen, had been diagnosed as having the same life threatening disease she herself had been diagnosed as having just within the past year. Her question was anything but inappropriate: "How much *is* enough?

Why do we have to face such enormously difficult trials? Why must they go on so long -- often one on top of the other? What's their place in any scheme of things we could call reasonable?

These are the tough questions for which there seem no easy, no truly satisfying answers. In general, however, there is a way to understand them.

For years, our family has enjoyed the challenge of working picture puzzles. In our home we have normally kept a puzzle on a small table, to be worked on as anyone had interest. Some have involved thousands of pieces. With several thousand pieces in disarray on that table, you can imagine how overwhelming it can seem! They're of every imaginable shape, and appear as if someone just randomly splattered them with various colors - intentionally without rhyme or reason.

The initial impression is this -- and you see how this speaks to the question we're addressing: by themselves alone, the pieces do not seem to have meaning.

Of course, in the case of picture puzzles, there's a way to access the meaning hidden in the separate pieces. Our family quickly learned the secret. All one had to do was to look at the complete picture on the front of the box. Having the entire picture in view provides the assurance that there is indeed meaning to these individual pieces.

Well, you say, this is obvious. But isn't this perhaps limited to the game of picture puzzles? Isn't this because the picture was there to begin with? Then that perfect picture was cut up into pieces. After all, it isn't really just random pieces.

I've discovered that life is very much like picture puzzles.

The analogy is quite appropriate. Let me explain further.

We can feel sadness for people who have no relationship with Jesus Christ. Not knowing Him is cause enough for sadness, but must we not ask whether they've had the privilege of having God's larger picture to guide them? If indeed they do not possess that picture, there is no way for them to make sense of those separate, confusing pieces of life they can and do see. From the very start, something is missing. Is it any wonder, then, that our society's educators and leaders -- psychiatrists, psychologists, professors and others -- can offer little if any comfort or hope, let alone direction? For apart from a personal relationship with Christ, they themselves have no idea what the larger, overall picture looks like, and hence have nothing to share with others.

How different it is for all who are trusting in the Lord Jesus Christ! In the Bible they have the complete picture from which to gain a perspective on all of life -- a picture clear and beautiful! There for all to read is God's plan for the forgiveness of sin, the gift of eternal life, the way of life abundant, yes, and with fullness of peace and joy!

Theologically, we refer to this overall picture as the sovereign, eternal plan of God. It was formulated, not in time, but in eternity past, with the ultimate goal God's own glory. It is a plan to make Him known as He manifests all of His marvelous attributes in heaven and on earth! Inasmuch as that plan contains everything that will ever come to pass in God's sovereign appointment, it is complete; it sets forth the complete picture. Still, except to the extent that God has chosen to reveal it in His Word, the detail of that plan is unknowable to us. In the revelation which is His Word we learn about sweeping things included in His overall purpose for the future, but are not given to know the times and details before they come to pass. As His purposes unfold, we shall be given understanding. This is His promise.

The events of life are like the pieces of a puzzle. God's sovereign plan is like the picture on the box. He has provided enough information about His sovereign plan to give us a picture of life as He intended it and as He shall fulfill it. Little is said in the Bible about the pieces. He leaves it to us -- within the means of day by day guidance which he provides -- to ponder how the pieces fit into the overall plan.

Sometimes a small piece of the puzzle makes little or no sense; it doesn't appear to fit anywhere at all. Nonetheless we can take it by faith that every piece indeed has its place. Why? Because God designed the picture, formulated the pieces as integral to the whole, and He Himself is working them all together to bring about the completed design.

It is the purpose of this book to help God's people (and those who may be seeking to know Him) to understand the big picture in order to make sense out of the little pieces that may be impeding spiritual progress. So we ask, What is it that God is doing? Where are we -- humanity in its present state, and especially we, believing individuals, where are we headed? Bringing it down to our personal lives, what is His purpose for me, for you? How do the decisions you and I make fit into His plan -- or do they? What relationship do they have to our inheritance and rewards in Christ? These are but a few of the important questions addressed in this book.

14

It is the author's desire that for all those who read these pages, this message will become for them a clear and certain aid in meeting their quest to know Him, and to be properly and assuredly oriented to His glorious plan.


G. Harry Leafe
Houston, Texas

# 1

# Discovering True Life

In the 1950's there was a television program called *This Is Your Life*, which became very popular, so much so that it has been recently reintroduced on prime time. The main idea of the program is to select an individual as the focal point, and then to bring in people from his or her past who upon their entrance are for awhile out of the individual's line of vision. They begin to speak about something from their past relationship, anticipating that the subject person would recognize them. The various people from the past are brought on in an order intended to convey an overview of the subject's life.

I remember first watching this program as a teenager, wondering what my life would look like over time if I were the subject, that is, what my life would look like if represented by a time line?  One way would be to draw a line on a piece of paper, set it off in five-year segments, and then begin to pinpoint specific events that highlight each segment.  When finished I would have a visual representation of the highlighted continuum of my life to the present.

The initial question is this: Of what does my life consist? If someone were to evaluate it, upon what basis would they do so?  These are important considerations, particularly in light of Paul's statement in 2 Corinthians 5:10: "For we must all appear before the judgment seat of Christ, that each one may be recompensed for his deeds in the body, according to what he has done, whether good or bad."

In order to understand the basis upon which God will judge our lives, we need to know the sense in which the word "life" is a biblical term standing for "soul."  In as much as this is the meaning, we must then ask, as we advance further, How is the term "soul" defined?

## The Meaning of "Soul"

As recorded in Matthew 16:24, our Lord told His disciples that to follow Him would be costly.  Here is how He put it: "If anyone wishes to come after Me, let him deny himself, and take up his cross, and follow Me." The statement is clearly in the context of discipleship. Earlier in His ministry Jesus had explained to Nicodemus the way of salvation from sin.  It was by faith in Him. As we shall note in our next segment, salvation from sin was not explained in terms of denying one's self, or in taking up one's cross, but rather in terms of simple faith in Christ. Consider John 3:16, "For God so loved the world, that He gave His only begotten Son, that whoever believes in Him should not perish but have eternal life." The Lord Jesus continued on to then explain about the cost of following Him.

The reason the issue is so critical is stated in Matthew 16:25, "For whoever wishes to save his life shall lose it, and whoever loses his life for My sake shall find it." From this statement it should be clear that Jesus is talking about the "desire" (motivation) of one's heart, and what issues from such motivation. In other words, it puts forth a contrast between a person trying to please himself and a person trying to please Christ.

In both instances where the word "life" appears in verse 25, it is a translation of the Greek term *psuche* (soul). In the progression of thought, this ties into the next verse, "For what will a man be profited, if he gains the whole world, and forfeits his own soul? Or what will a man give in exchange for his soul?"

When we consider a person's life (or soul) as the term is used in this context, it will be helpful to determine a more precise meaning, especially since we do not commonly use the term "soul" in ordinary speech. Of just what does one's life (soul) consist? And in what sense can one exchange it for something? And this something for which it may be exchanged -- what does it have to do with the event mentioned by Paul, "For we must all appear before the judgment seat of Christ"?

Notice Jesus' complementing statement in verse 27, "For the Son of Man is going to come in the glory of His

Father with His angels; and will then recompense every
man according to his deeds."

The term "recompense" (Gr. *apodidomai*), means "to
render or give back what is due." The Greek-English
lexicon of Arndt and Gingrich as well as that of Liddell
and Scott, agree as to the meaning of the term -- that
whatever is due may relate to either good or bad. If a
person is to receive something from the Lord that is *due*
him, whether good or bad, certainly this does not
concern salvation from sin (cf. Rom. 4:1-5), but rather to
something that indeed can be earned. So just what does
Paul have in mind?

Paul's words both in 2 Cor. 5:10 and Eph. 6:8 carry the
same truth. In the phrase, ". . . that each one may be
recompensed for his deeds in the body" (the Corinthian
passage), he uses the Greek word *komizo* (recompense),
the same as in the Ephesian passage, "knowing that
whatever good thing each one does, *he will receive back
(komizo) from the Lord*" (italics mine).

The concept of receiving a wage due one is even stron-
ger with *komizo* than with *apodidomai* (recompense)!
Certainly "to get for one's self by earning" is not related
to salvation from sin, since we are told that "For *by
grace* you have been saved through faith, and that not of
yourselves; *it is the gift of God; not as a result of works*,
that no one should boast (Eph. 2:8-9, italics mine).

Whatever comprises one's life (soul) becomes the basis
of the wage due or reward earned. We've already
observed that our works play a part in the transaction.
But the term "works" itself seems to include the total

product of one's life. Helpfully, the term can be expanded to include other components of a specific nature. For example, our Lord said, ". . . every careless word that men shall speak, they shall render account for it in the day of judgment (Matt. 12:36). Further, the Bible speaks to the matter of our thinking, or reasoning processes, when it says, "Therefore, do not go on passing judgment before the time, but wait until the Lord comes who will . . . disclose *the motives of men's hearts*; and then each man's praise will come to him from God" (1 Cor. 4:5, italics mine).

Before giving a final definition to the term soul as our Lord used it in Matthew 16 and elsewhere, it is important to remember that words are often used in different ways. For example, simply looking at how human beings are constituted, we conclude that they are basically two-part beings. We are both material and non-material. To describe various functions of our non-material being, very often the term soul is used. Other words are used in this same way, for example, spirit, mind and heart. Like soul, these terms are used to describe the various functions of our non-material self.

Sometimes, however, a term can be used to describe the whole of something, and it is in this sense that the term soul is used in Matthew 16; it describes the whole of a person's life. When used in this way it can be defined as *the total temporal expression of human life.* It is what we shall refer to as "soul-life."

Soul-life has three essential components: thoughts, words, actions. Together, the sum of these make up our lives as lived during our time upon earth. It is obvious that some of our thoughts are proper, some are not. The same with words and actions.

Keep in mind that what we are endeavoring to present in these pages is the big picture of God's program for training His children. We are not discussing the lives of unbelievers, but believers, and what commonly is referred to as *discipleship*. Theologically speaking, the term is *sanctification*.

## With Eternity's Values in Mind?

People have different ideas about that of which life consists. Some think an abundance of material possessions, for to them this means importance, security, often a sense of "I've got the resources; I can handle anything!" Others see education and its attendant honors as the essence of life. Still others think relationships with other people provide the key to life abundant. It may well be that many of these same people give some place, however superficially, to God. But is it the proper place; should He not be central to their lives?

The real problem is one of priority, God's imperative place which Jesus taught His disciples. To follow Him would mean putting Him first. In whatever we think, say, or do, to put Him first has more than temporal value; it has eternal value. Conversely, the thinking, saying or doing that puts ourselves first has temporal value only, not eternal value.

Paul set forth this principle in his admonition to slaves in Ephesians 6. They were to serve their masters ". . . in the sincerity of your heart, as to Christ; not by way of eyeservice, as men-pleasers, but as slaves of Christ, doing the will of God from the heart" (vvs. 5-6).

Now, having a desire to gratify *self* comes quite naturally, as most of us would grant. We are sinners, and as such are self-serving. Although the tendency will always remain, growing in Christ will make us less so. Paul warned the Philippians about this: "Do nothing from selfishness or empty conceit, but with humility of mind let each of you regard one another as more important than himself; do not merely look out for your own personal interests, but also for the interests of others" (2:3-4).

Seeking to *save one's life*, as Jesus put it, is to be temporally oriented. Losing one's life for Christ's sake is to be oriented to eternity. This, as we shall see, lends significance to Jesus' question, "What will a man give in exchange for his soul?"

Keeping in mind that "soul" stands for "soul-life," how might this truth be illustrated? Is there a way to quantify our soul-life? Let's assign it a certain time-value, maybe seventy years. And let's give it a dollar value, perhaps $1,440,000.00 (an annual income of $36,000.00 for forty years). On this scale of values, how much of one's money would be invested in people, places and things that have only temporal value -- the consequence of such investment having no more than temporal worth? In other words, what portion of one's investment ought to relate to life in earthly time, how much to life in eternity? Have you considered life in terms of this scale of values? Let's return to Jesus' concept of saving or losing one's life.

## When Our Soul Shall Be Required of Us

We are daily told by well-meaning people that we have lots of unmet needs that rightfully are to be taken care of. The suggestion is that unless and until these personal needs are met, we cannot adequately minister to those around us. We are to love ourselves, feel good about ourselves, grow in self-esteem and the sense of self-worth. *Then* we can reach beyond ourselves to serve others. *Then* we can extend our love to other people.

The Bible, however, never speaks in these terms. First, we are never told to love ourselves. Assumably, we do this quite naturally (cf. Eph. 5:29; Matt. 22:39). Further, we are never told to be concerned about personal needs. On the contrary, Jesus taught His disciples that when they followed that philosophy of life -- putting self first -- they were actually doing what unbelievers were by nature disposed to do (cf. Matt. 6:32). As followers of Him, they (and we) are to "seek first His kingdom and His righteousness; and all these things shall be added to you" (Matt. 6:33).

God gave a similar answer to Paul who prayed for deliverance from a personal affliction. In this case, God's reply to his perceived need was, "My grace is sufficient for you, for power is perfected in weakness" (2 Cor. 12:9).

Sometimes He chooses to deliver us, sometimes not. Ultimately it is His sovereign will that matters. Ours is to seek first His kingdom and righteousness, and then as He sees fit He appoints for us that which will meet our true needs.

Doesn't this really strike at the heart of the problem? Are we going to occupy ourselves with those things that are merely temporal, or are we going to pursue that which is eternal?

Note how the Lord Jesus speaks to this. After telling His disciples not to be concerned about themselves but rather about pleasing and serving God, He related the blessedness of the Father's concern, how He will take care of them.

The world cannot see it this way, for to suggest that one not be concerned for himself does not make sense. Who, if not ourselves, will? But, contrary to the world's reasoning, God's plan for His children is the divinely designated way to true happiness and fulfillment in this life. Abundant living is truly there for us, but only as it is found in a personal, living relationship with the Lord Jesus Christ (cf. Jn. 10:10).

To further clarify His point, Jesus told a story (Lk. 12:13-21). The subject of the story is a business man who at that time had great wealth. Moreover, his business continued to prosper. What will he do with so much? Self-centered in his thinking, his words and actions consistently focused in the same direction. His reasoning was as follows: "This is what I will do: I will tear down my barns and build larger ones, and there I will store all my grain and my goods. And I will say to my soul, 'Soul, you have many goods laid up for many years to come; take your ease, eat, drink and be merry'" (vss. 18-19).

Sound reasonable?   Take a look at God's response:
"You fool! This very night your soul is required of you;
and now who will own what you have prepared?" (vvs
20).   Do you identify the basic problem?   He had
invested his life in that which had only temporal value,
only transient worth.   And when he died all he had
acquired was gone!

Apply this to those who follow Him, who seek to do His
bidding.  They, too, must not overlook the lesson: "So is
the man who lays up treasure *for himself*, and is not rich
toward God" (vs. 21, italics mine).  A person can be rich
in the world's eyes, yet not rich toward God.  Or he can
be rich toward God, although not rich in the world's
value system.  This is what Jesus meant by saving or
losing our lives.

# 2

# Saved And Being Saved

In the Holy Land, the Town of Caesarea Philippi is situated on the southern slopes of Mount Hermon, located north of the Sea of Galilee. When the Greeks came into the area following the conquest of Alexander the Great, they established a shrine for one of their gods, Pan. These Greeks believed that Hades was located beneath the mountain area where the shrine to Pan was established; and inasmuch as the easternmost source of the Jordan River is found at this same location, flowing out from there, they also believed it to be the source of life. Herein is an interesting connection. We can believe that Jesus brought the disciples to this spot for a very important reason!

It was near this pagan site that the Lord Jesus asked His

disciples the penetrating question, "Who do people say that the Son of Man is?" (Matt. 16:13). Their reply accurately reflected what the people generally considered to be the case: "Some say John the Baptist; and others, Elijah; but still others Jeremiah, or one of the prophets" (vs. 14).

Standing in the midst of what represented fallen mankind's understanding of the essence of life, He was now going to take them the next step in their understanding of the plan of God and the real meaning of life. To do this He must first show them their own mistaken views.

Jesus directed the question straight to them: "But who do you say that I am?" Expectedly, Simon Peter acted as spokesman for the group, "Thou art the Christ, the Son of the living God" (vs. 16).

We can make two important observations: First, the disciples had not come to their understanding about Christ on their own. Jesus affirmed this: "...flesh and blood did not reveal this to you, but My Father who is in heaven" (vs. 17). Second, it is upon Himself (as stated in Peter's confession) "...I will build My church, and the gates of Hades shall not overpower it" (vs. 18). Peter was a rock, but Jesus Himself was the true foundation upon which the church was to be built, not Peter.

The disciples are being brought along in their understanding of life from God's point of view. From the context we learn that man's understanding, quite different from God's, is built upon a system we call

*Humanism.* And whether in our Lord's day, or our own, *Humanism* represents mankind's self-devised search for life.

As they journeyed from Caesarea Philippi, the Lord continued to instruct them about Himself and their relationship to Him. He continued to build new meaning into the term *life*: "...whoever wishes to save his life will lose it, and whoever loses his life for My sake shall find it" (Matt. 16:25).

Their journey ultimately brought them to Jerusalem where they would celebrate the Feast of Booths. It was an important occasion, particularly, as it turned out, for the disciples. For on the last day of the feast, a startling thing happened. Jesus stood up in the midst of the great crowd of people and made a loud proclamation. John records the event in this way: "Now on the last day, the great day of the feast, Jesus stood and cried out saying 'If any man is thirsty, let him come to Me and drink. He who believes in Me, as the Scripture said, out of his innermost being shall flow rivers of living water'" (Jn. 7:37-38).

In Jesus' announcement the two approaches to life are finally sorted out. What man desperately and falsely seeks at the waters of Humanism, is declared to reside, truly, in Jesus Christ, and to be available to all those who place their faith in Him. We know now something more of what life consists.

## Praise For A Living Hope

Before the advent of the Holy Spirit and the beginning

experiences of New Covenant blessings, Peter, like the other disciples, had a difficult time trying to put two and two together spiritually. Jesus explained this difficulty to Peter when He said, "What I do you do not realize now, but you shall understand hereafter" (Jn. 13:7). This inability had existed throughout the whole three and a half years that he and the others had spent with the Lord. But things were to be different in the future. That same evening Jesus said to all of them, "But, when He, the Spirit of truth, comes, He will guide you into all the truth; for He will not speak on His own initiative, but whatever He hears, He will speak; and He will disclose to you what is to come. He shall glorify Me; for He shall take of Mine, and shall disclose it to you" (Jn. 16:13-14).

By the time he wrote his first epistle, Peter had put it all together. He had come to understand the connection between soul-life, rivers of living water, and faith in Christ. Moreover, he had come to understand that soul-life has a relationship to the events of time, although always with a view to eternity. As he addresses the subject, he begins where Jesus began with him: God's saving grace and the hope (confidence) that it brings to those who believe in Christ.

Listen to Peter: "Blessed be the God and Father of our Lord Jesus Christ, who according to His great mercy *has caused us to be born again* to a living hope through the resurrection of Jesus Christ from the dead" (1 Pet. 1:3, italics mine). Salvation is the work of God. Man's inability to respond to the revelation of God (cf. Rom. 3:9-18; 8:5-8), necessitates a work of God's grace in the heart if any are to be saved. At the moment of salvation, the truth of the Gospel of Christ is revealed and through the Holy Spirit faith to believe is granted. Thus, through this transaction, a person is *caused to be born again to a living hope.*

We need to distinguish Peter's view of "hope" from that of the world. Peter does not imply that hope has some degree of uncertainty. From the biblical perspective, hope expresses certainty -- the confidence of hope engendered by the Holy Spirit and grounded upon God's sure Word. Our Sovereign, all-powerful God will do as He has decreed!

Our salvation from the penalty of sin and salvation's related hope is with a view to an inheritance that is to be revealed in the future. Moreover, we read that it is an inheritance "imperishable and undefiled and will not fade away, reserved in heaven for you" (1 Pet. 1:4). It is an inheritance for us who believe in Christ. And the question is not whether we will *get there* to receive it, but rather *how much* of it we will receive. Receiving a full inheritance is conditional, as we shall see in the ongoing chapters.

Here is a fundamental point that must not be underestimated. Once we have been saved from the penalty of sin through faith in Christ, it is not possible for us to be lost again. Why? Because we are not saved on the basis of our own goodness or works, but by the redemptive provision of God's unmerited grace. Even faith to believe is not generated on our own, but too is a gift of God (cf. Eph. 2:8-9; Phil. 1:28). This being so, what is it that keeps me saved? My goodness as a believer? My Christian works? No! The power of God and that alone!  Salvation is not preserved by good works!

Now look carefully at Peter's word in verse 5: "...who are protected by the power of God through faith...." The word "protected" is a translation of the Greek *phroureo*. There are some important things about the way this word is used here.  First, it is a verb expressed in the present tense; it concerns something continuing on in the present time.  Use of the passive voice indicates that it is something being done to us.  Of equal importance, *phroureo* uniquely means "to keep in a state of security." That aspect is vital!

What is underscored is that we who are believers in Christ are being kept in a state of secured salvation by the power of God, and all this is with a view to an inheritance still future.  No wonder Peter exclaims, "In this you greatly rejoice" (vs. 6).  What a hope is ours! What security is ours!

## The Necessity of Trials

Recall once more that Peter had come to understand that soul-life has a connection with events in time. Midway in verse 6 he begins to explain that connection. Note the qualifying phrase attached to "In this you greatly rejoice": while rejoicing in the inheritance awaiting us in heaven, we meet Peter's "even though now for a little while, *if* necessary..." (italics mine). The conditional "if", as used here, in the Greek language assumes reality.  That is, we are to expect trials as a necessary reality in Christian living, a testing by trials, as stated in verse 7, and this has to do with "the proof of our faith." What, then, is the connection?

## Proof of Faith

The trials Peter has in mind are designed by our heavenly Father to prove our faith (not destroy it!). To be sure, trials also demonstrate lack of faith. But the issue here is the *proof* (Gr. *dokimion*) of our faith, said to be "more precious than gold which perishes." The clear implication is that gold, in this analogy, has only temporal value, while the *proof* of faith has eternal value. This is further expressed in the outcome -- such proven faith results in "praise and glory and honor at the revelation of Jesus Christ."

Another important point needs to be made with regard to the *proof* of our faith. We will get into this more later, but Peter uses *proof* of faith to indicate what the Bible also calls *good works*. Our evaluations and responses to the concerns of life will either issue from faith in the provisions of God's grace, or in our own self-sufficiency. In either case, a work is produced. If the work issues from our faith in God, it is a *good work* (cf. Rom. 14:23b; Eph. 2:10). It is *proof* of faith. All our works, good and bad, will be "tested by fire" at the judgment seat of Christ (cf. 1 Corinthians 3:10-15). The judgment by fire is to test the *quality* of our works (vs. 13). *Good works* (*proof* of faith) become the basis for reward (vs. 14). This is precisely what Peter has in mind when he says that our "*proof* of faith" (*good works*) will be "tested by fire", and having passed the test will result in "praise and glory and honor" (reward). And it will happen at "the revelation of Jesus Christ" (the judgment seat). To put it another way, our faith is proven in time, but that proof is demonstrated and rewarded in the future -- at the judgment seat of Christ.

Can we believe in and actually serve someone we've never seen? That, you may say, takes real faith! Yes it does, and that's exactly what Peter insists is our present condition. Notice how he frames it in verse 8: "though you have not seen Him, you love Him, and though you do not see Him now, but believe in Him, you greatly rejoice with joy inexpressible and full of glory."

Clearly, then, the trials we experience in life are designed to test our faith, and of necessity the testing involves our thoughts, words and actions. This being the case, will we then evaluate our circumstances on the basis of God's Word -- a biblical world view, or on some other basis, whatever that might be? Will the intent of our words be to minister to and build up those around us? Will the purpose of our actions be to demonstrate our faith in Christ? If these responses issue from faith, then they become what Peter calls *proof* of faith. And it is the *proof* of faith that will be demonstrated and rewarded at "the revelation of Jesus Christ", an event of great importance; and as we shall see later, one that plays a vital role in the development of this book.

**The Salvation of Your Soul**

Recall from Chapter 1 the discussion about our ability to save our soul-life. We learned that the issue is one of *sanctification*, not of salvation from the penalty of sin. We also learned that our soul-life consists of our thoughts, words and actions. Some of these issue from faith, others do not. Those of faith have eternal value, while the others have only temporal significance. Recall, too, that our Lord stated, "Whoever wishes to save his life (Gr. *psuche*) shall lose it; but whoever loses his life (Gr. *psuche*) for My sake, he is the one who will save it" (Luke 9:24).

The term *save* (Gr. *sozo*) means "to rescue, liberate, preserve, deliver." The question is this: What did our Lord mean when He used this term? He taught us that in some manner we can exchange the temporal experiences of human life for that which is eternal: "Lay up for yourselves treasures in heaven" (Matt. 6:20); "What will a man give in exchange for his soul?" (Matt. 16:26). And in so doing, we actually *save* our soul-life from time to eternity (cf. Lk. 12:20-21). Clearly Jesus meant *to deliver* our soul-life, which also happens to be the primary meaning of the term in the New Testament.

But what can Peter add from *his* understanding of what Jesus taught about this matter? How does *this* salvation work itself out in life? In the passage before us notice how he has developed a connection between "an inheritance" (vs. 4), "a salvation" (vs. 5), and the "praise and glory and honor" (vs. 7) -- all of which are associated with "the revelation of Jesus Christ" (vs. 7). The "inheritance" is what awaits us in heaven. "Praise and glory and honor" reflects the reception of our portion of that inheritance. But what about "a salvation?"

It is difficult for grace oriented believers to think in terms of earning anything from God. Certainly salvation from the penalty of sin is a free gift of God's grace. However, Peter now tells us that we obtain (Gr. *komizo*) as the outcome of our faith "the salvation of our souls" (vs. 9). Clearly the salvation of verse 5 is the same as verse 9, "a salvation ready to be revealed in the last time." Recall from chapter 1 that *komizo* means "to receive something that is due, or to get for oneself by earning."

The point is clear: our share in the inheritance is determined by that portion of our soul-life that is saved or delivered into eternity. And *that* salvation is demonstrated by our good works or, as Peter put it, *proof* of faith. We receive inheritance on the basis of our *demonstrated* faith (good works). And that is what "salvation of the soul" is all about!

# 3

## Is Your Faith Real?

**R**ecently I was watching the evening news on television, and during the first commercial break a beautiful woman appeared and exclaimed, "I've had it with reality; I want illusion!" What did she mean? It was a come-on.

Although she was talking about her appearance and how a certain brand of cosmetics could make her look like something she was not, I was suddenly struck by the philosophy of life represented by her statement (not hers, of course, but put in her mouth by the cosmetic company's ad people). People *do* live in a world of illusion, whether they are aware of it or not. People *do* mask the reality of their lives so that others will see something other than what is really there. Every one of us tends to live behind a facade of our own devising. All too often our lives betray an altogether unreal quality, a certain inauthenticity.

What others see in us -- is this really what's there? What are we leading others to believe we are? In reality, are the true characteristics of our lives the fruit of the Spirit, or are we merely mastering the technique of pretense -- *emulating* Christlikeness in outward behavior only, without the conforming, inner work of the Spirit? Are we more concerned that people *think* we are spiritual, despite our knowing we are not?

What about you? Has your life become a life of illusion? Is or is not your life an authentic enactment of your faith -- really, now? What answer fits you best?

## Faith That Works

In 1 Peter 1:7, the Apostle wrote "that the proof of your faith, being more precious than gold which is perishable, even though tested by fire, may be found to result in praise and glory and honor at the revelation of Jesus Christ." Notice once again that it is the *proof* of our faith that is more precious than gold. Why? Because it will result in "praise and honor and glory" at the revelation of Jesus Christ. Proof of faith, as we have seen, is an expression for what the Bible calls good works, works which become the basis of our share in the inheritance in Christ.

The term "that" which begins the verse indicates purpose and takes us back to the statement of verse 6, "...even though now for a little while, if necessary (*which it is!*), you have been distressed by various trials." Here is an interesting connection. Our faith is proven in the context of life's normal activities and circumstances. Within the activities and circumstances the trials or tests of our faith appear. To repeat an earlier statement, how we evaluate and respond to the concerns of life will either issue from faith in the provisions of God's grace, or from faith in our own sufficiency. What results -- our thoughts, words and actions, will betray the real intent of our heart, and thus the reality of our faith, or the lack thereof.

## The Value of Proven Faith

It was well-known to Peter that a clear relationship exists between how we handle the tests of our faith and our inheritance in Christ. A proper faith-response proves our faith, and the proof of our faith results in reward and inheritance -- the salvation of our soul. But as clearly as Peter has stated these truths, it does not present the total picture.

James, the writer of the epistle that bears his name, himself the half-brother of our Lord, was also aware of the relationship between trials and faith, and how proper faith responses are a part of the development process that matures and completes the child of God, and prepares him for his inheritance.

Even though he did not come to believe in his elder brother as Messiah until after Jesus had been raised from the dead, James had been exposed to what He had taught on many occasions (cf. Matt. 12:46-50; 13:55, 56; Jn. 2:12; 7:3, 5). Can it be assumed then that James understood about soul-life and the concept of the salvation of the soul as Peter had? Lets take a look.

A close look at his epistle will reveal that James uses the term "save" (Gr. *sozo*) five times. But not once does he use it in a context dealing with salvation from the penalty of sin. In fact there is not even a hint that there may be an unbeliever in his audience, and nineteen times he refers to his readers as brethren. The book is really a handbook on Christian living.

Let's look at two of his usages of the term save. The first is in 1:21, where he urges his readers to "receive the word implanted, which is able to *save your souls*" (italics mine). Notice the connection that he makes between salvation of the soul and obedience to the Word as he continues, "And prove yourselves to be doers of the word, and not merely hearers, who delude themselves" (vs. 22). To James, a life of faith is a life lived in obedience to the Word of God. It is a life that issues in a product -- proven faith.

"My brethren, do not hold your faith in our glorious Lord Jesus Christ with an attitude of personal favoritism," James says (2:1). As believers in Christ we all have faith. It was a gift to us at the moment of our regeneration by the Spirit of God. But just having it is not an end in itself. It must be exercised to have value, but exercised appropriately within the normal circumstances of life. James offers a good example in the next verses when he relates the exercise of our faith to the way we tend to judge people.

Loving our neighbor as ourself means that we treat all people equitably. Because one has wealth and prestige as judged by our culture does not give the right to neglect one who is less fortunate. In fact, when any of us does so it indicates we are not living in faithful obedience to God's Word, which tells us to love our neighbor as ourself!

This commandment, to love our neighbor as ourself, is the second of the two great commandments as delineated by our Lord. The first being to love God with all our heart, soul and mind. These two commandments comprise what James variously calls The Perfect Law (1:25); The Law of Liberty (1:25); and The Royal Law (2:8). They touch every aspect and moment of life, and teach us that our lives should be lived as those who will be judged by them (2:12).

Having developed this progression of obedient faith -- a faithful obedience to God's Word, fleshed out in the circumstances of life within the parameters of the Royal Law, a vitally important question is asked, "What use is it, my brethren, if a man says he has faith, but he has no works? Can that faith save him? The answer demanded by the text is a firm *no*. But save in what sense? Recall that James has already said that a reception of the "implanted word" ultimately issues in the salvation of the soul. By reception James means more than just hearing it or believing it to be true. He means receiving it with the thought of living in faithful obedience to it, the results of which are works of faith.

The context is one of judgment. In the future the Believer will not face judgment for sin -- Christ died for our sins. Therefore, the judgment before us must be the judgment seat of Christ (2 Cor. 5:10). And it is at the judgment seat of Christ that our works of faith will be rewarded. They actually become the basis of our portion of the inheritance in Christ (we will develop this in a later chapter). Since our works of faith represent our soul-life (we developed this in the first two chapters), we are, by our obedient responses, saving our souls.

Suppose, as James is doing, that a person says he lives by faith. How are we to know that what he is saying is actually true? Can faith alone save his soul (soul-life)? It is important to repeat that James is not talking about salvation from the penalty of sin, rather he is talking about the same thing Peter talked about when he said that our share in the inheritance is determined by that portion of our soul-life that is saved or delivered into eternity. And *that* salvation is demonstrated by our good works or, *proof* of faith. We receive inheritance on the basis of our *demonstrated* faith (good works). And that is what "salvation of the soul" is all about! Just having faith without obedient responses through works is not enough.

Every believer in Christ has faith, but it is what is produced by that faith that gives it its reality and value. There is no better example than that of Abraham offering his son Isaac as a sacrifice (2:21-24). Abraham had faith. God had earlier proclaimed him righteous on the basis of it -- apart from any works whatsoever (Gen. 15:6; Rom. 4:1-25). Now, many years later, in the providence of God he is being placed in a situation where his faith is to be "proven."

Abraham's son, Isaac, was the individual through whom God would confirm the covenant. He was the only son of promise. What would Abraham do? How would he reason? Would his evaluation of himself and his circumstances issue from faith in the revelation of God? Would his thoughts, words and actions *prove* the reality his faith?

The writer of Hebrews provides some important insight into this event: "By faith Abraham, when he was tested, offered up Isaac; and he who had received the promises was offering up his only begotten son; it was he to whom it was said, 'In Isaac your descendants shall be called.' He considered that God is able to raise men even from the dead" (11:17-19). Please note that Abraham thought "biblically." His actions were based on faith in his "biblical reasonings." In a word, his works of faith proved the reality of his faith. He was justified (in the sense of being vindicated) before men -- not before God. Remember, that had occurred earlier.

Therefore, James arrives at the conclusion: "For just as the body without the spirit is dead, as also faith without works is dead" (vs. 26). That is, such faith, in terms of the salvation of the soul, is as useless as a dead body!

## Be Prepared For The Pop Quizzes!

When I was a student at Dallas Seminary, my Greek professor was famous for his daily "pop quizzes." Not to have a pop quiz was a rare exception! It kept you on your toes. And we never knew what form they would take. One day I might have been asked to write out vocabulary words. On another I might have been called upon to recite the Greek alphabet. And still on another I might have been invited to the chalkboard to write out and diagram a sentence from the Greek New Testament. The important point was this: be prepared. It was not a question of "if" a quiz was coming, only "when!"

James actually begins his epistle with this same thought: "Count it all joy, my brethren, when you encounter various trials" (1:2). With James the matter of trials or tests of faith (what I like to call "pop quizzes") was not a matter of "if" either, only "when."

But why are we to "count it all joy?" What is the basis for such a response? It is our knowledge of the relationship between faith, tests of faith, maturity, and our inheritance in Christ. "Knowing," he says, "that the testing of your faith produces endurance. And let endurance have its perfect result, that you may be perfect and complete, lacking in nothing" (vvs. 3-4).

It should be very obvious by this time that the tests of our faith come in the normal activities and circumstances of life. In that regard we can say that everything we face in life is a test of faith. Why? Because we are called upon to evaluate the basis of it. Will these words then edify and minister grace to the hearers? Or we may be called upon to perform some action. Will it reflect love for God and/or our neighbor? In other words, will we make a faith-response? Will our thoughts, words and actions prove the reality of our faith?

It is indeed unfortunate that almost every English translation reads "the testing of your faith" in verse 3. There is no verb or participle in the Greek text. And it is the same exact phrase that appears in 1 Pet. 1:7, which is consistently translated as "the proof of your faith."

Only in the translation, *Today's English Version*, have I been able to locate an accurate rendering of verse 3: "For you know that when your faith succeeds in facing such trials, the result is the ability to endure."

The point to be emphasized is this: it is not the trials that result in endurance. It is not gritting one's teeth and hanging in there through the difficulties of life. It is, like a math test, working the problems successfully -- passing the test, not just taking it!

Proven faith, according to James, results in a product -- steadfast endurance (Gr. *hupomone*). The term means "mental toughness, stick-to-itiveness." It is a character quality without which we are unable to successfully run "the race of life" (cf. Heb. 12:1). Without it we cannot become mature in Christ. The term "perfect" in verse 4 is the common New Testament expression for maturity. And ultimately, without it we will not obtain a full reward. The phrase "lacking nothing" is built off the same Greek root word as is the term "inheritance."

Let some closing comments from the apostle Paul help reinforce the idea of this chapter. In Rom. 5:1-5, he tells us about our new standing before God: "Having been justified by faith, we have peace with God through our Lord Jesus Christ" (vs. 1). He then says that through our relationship with Christ, we have "obtained our introduction by faith into this grace in which we stand; and we exult in the hope of God" (vs. 2). Certainly we can all appreciate the position we enjoy in the sphere of God's grace and the provisions of His grace that sustain us day by day. And we all rejoice greatly in the confidence that we will one day share in

His glory.  But Paul does not stop there.

Now he states the same truth that James and Peter told us about.    Namely, that "...we also exult in our tribulations, knowing..." (vs. 3a).  The Greek term for tribulations is *thelipsis*, and refers to the "stresses and pressures of life."  Rejoice over the stress and pressure of my job?  You've got to be kidding!  No, he is not kidding.  And the reason is because we are expected to know something -- "...that tribulation (stress and pressure) brings about perseverance" (vs. 3b).  Wow! Stress and pressure are what James would refer to as "various trials."   And we would understand that Paul does not mean that these things in themselves produce perseverance, but rather that *a proper response* to them produces perseverance.   By the way, this is the same word (Gr. *hupomone*) that James uses.    To Paul, handling stress and pressure successfully (on the basis of faith) produces steadfast endurance.  To James, our faith is proven when we handle the various trials of life successfully (on the basis of faith), and as a result steadfast endurance is produced.

Notice the progression that follows: "and perseverance (brings about), proven character; and proven character (brings about), hope; and hope does not disappoint" (vvs. 4-5).  Isn't this the same progression that James wrote about?  Doesn't the salvation of our soul involve a process of growth in faith?  Aren't we really being trained and matured like children?

# 4.

## Its For Your Own Good!

When we encounter trials and tests of our faith, whether suddenly or -- as in every life -- regularly, James says that we are to consider it as "total joy." In making that assertion he assumes a certain frame of reference. First, that we understand the dynamic relationship between the tests of our faith and maturity, and secondly, that our maturity in Christ relates to our inheritance in Christ.

In the case of personal growth, to become a mature person requires training and development through a growth process that will take one from being an immature babe to a fully mature, productive adult. The process requires parental oversight and guidance. And both the Scriptures and experience teach us that the process can be quite an ordeal!

The Proverbs tell us that children are naturally foolish. Solomon put it this way: "Foolishness is bound up in the heart of a child" (Prov. 22:15). In general they are rebellious and require discipline. In fact, the second half of verse fifteen tells us that "The rod of discipline will remove it (foolishness) far from him."

Because children are foolish, they very often do not listen to the wisdom and instruction of their parents. The american author Mark Twain made a good point of this when he wrote, "When I was a boy of fourteen, my father was so ignorant I could hardly stand to have the old man around. But when I got to be twenty-one, I was astonished at how much he had learned in seven years."

It happens in the spiritual realm as well. Both the Old and New Testaments are replete with metaphors that picture God as a loving Father faithfully training His children. The point is so clear it does not need to be argued. Even the process and methods that He uses to train us are spelled out. Do you know what they are? Have you ever tried to relate the events of your life to this growth process? Do you see a relationship between the momentary tests of your faith that James talks about and God's overall training program? How about the stress and pressure that Paul speaks about in Romans 5:3 -- how does that fit into the process?

## Learning From Past Experiences

The Jewish Christians who lived in and around

Jerusalem really had it rough. Imagine being raised in a culture dominated by the Law of Moses, where strict conformity to Mosaic legislation was expected -- and even demanded. Imagine yourself identifying with a new religious group that was considered to be anti-Jewish and anti-Law of Moses, a group that believed its leader to be the promised Messiah. Your boss has told you that you are no longer needed. The shops in town no longer want to do business with you. You and your family are treated as outcasts from society.

You are not alone in your experience. Many others have also chosen to follow the Lord Jesus Christ as their Messiah. Many of them have experienced the seizure of their properties, some have even been thrown into prison. For a good while now you and the others have accepted your tribulations joyfully. You have tried to help each other the best you could. The Apostle Paul has also been a great help. Not long ago he was able to raise a large amount of money from among your gentile brethren. It certainly helped a lot of people.

But "Enough is enough!" you say. "Surely Jesus should have returned by this time, it's been thirty years!" "How long must we endure these hardships?"

A short time later you begin to notice that some of your friends in the Church are no longer there when you meet. You've heard that they've gone back to the old system. Maybe that's not a bad idea. Surely you would be welcomed back. Your old boss may be so glad to see you come to your senses that he might give you back your old job. You won't stop believing in Jesus as your Messiah and Savior, you reason, you'll just go through the motions of the Law. You might even lead some of them to believe in Christ!

What I have just described is the situation of the recipients of the letter to the Hebrews. In the letter the writer argues that what they are defecting from is far superior to what they are going back to. Jesus Christ is superior revelation (1:1-4); He is superior to Angels, beings held in high regard by the Jews (1:5-2:18); He is superior to Moses the Law giver (3:1-6); He is superior to Aaron the Law interpreter (4:14ff); and His priesthood is superior to that of the old Jewish order (7:1-28). He demonstrates the superiority of the work of Christ by contrasting the New Covenant with the Old (8:1-13); the New Sanctuary with the Old (9:1-10); and the New Sacrifice with the Old (9:11-10:18).

But carefully woven within his argument is a picture that is intended to bring fear to the hearts of the strongest of men. Simply stated, the picture is this: those who are believers in Christ are obligated to live in faithful obedience to the directives of the New Covenant. Just because the penalty of our sin was borne by Christ on the cross does not mean that there are no consequences for sin. Just as the children of Israel forfeited their inheritance because of unbelief -- "the word they heard did not profit them, because it was not united by faith in those who heard" (Heb. 4:2), we face that same possibility. It can happen to us the same way it happened to them. Thus the writer warns, "Take care, brethren, lest there be in any one of you an evil, unbelieving heart, in falling away from the living God" (3:12).

But what are we to do? "Encourage one another day after day, . . .lest any one of you be hardened by the deceitfulness of sin" (3:13). The Hebrews had failed. At the beginning their works of faith demonstrated an obedient walk with God. But now there are no works of faith. And there is no steadfast endurance (remember that James and Paul have said that steadfast endurance comes about as a result of an obedient faith). Even under the Old Covenant believers endured great hardship -- including the loss of life -- in order to lay hold of the promise (Heb. 11). What about you? Have the stress and pressure and afflictions of life caused you to become disoriented to the plan of God? That's what happened to the Hebrews.

Some years ago I took flying lessons to obtain a pilots license. During the course of the instruction, I was taught (by demonstration) how easy it is to become disoriented in flight when you do not have an outside object with which to orient yourself -- like when flying through a bank of clouds. It is possible to believe that you are ascending when in fact you are descending. You may believe that you are flying right-side up when really you are up-side down. They only way to survive is to trust your instruments. No matter what your senses tell you, you must trust your instruments.

The Hebrews became disoriented "flying through the clouds of life." They were "flying" according to their senses. They never checked the "instruments" -- God's Word!

## A Proper Orientation

"Since we have so great a cloud of witnesses surrounding us, let us also lay aside every encumbrance and the sin which so easily entangles us, and let us run with endurance the race that is set before us, fixing our eyes on Jesus the author and perfecter of faith, who for the joy set before Him endured the cross, despised the shame, and has sat down at the right hand of the throne of God" (Heb. 12:1-2).

"Don't let anything keep you from the finish line," the writer says. "Many others have done it, and you can too. But to make it takes endurance, and you must keep your eyes firmly fixed on the finish line. Great reward awaits those who run the race successfully." But then, if it is so simple, what happened to the Hebrews? They forgot something!

What they forgot is at once both simple and profound: "You have forgotten the exhortation which is addressed to you as sons, 'My son, do not regard lightly the discipline of the Lord, nor faint when you are reproved by Him; for those whom the Lord loves He disciplines, and He scourges every son whom He receives'" (12:5). It is a quote from Proverbs 3:11-12. Everything they were experiencing in life was related to this statement. They had failed to orient themselves on the basis of it. Their regression from maturity back to being babes again (5:11-6:12), their lack of steadfast endurance, and their potential loss of inheritance, all resulted from a lack of application of this truth!

God is training us as His children. Everything we

experience in life is a part of that training process. It is the very same thing James and Paul spoke about. The circumstances of our lives (stress, pressure, tests of faith) are intended to mature our faith and equip us to receive our inheritance. They accomplish that as long as we handle them correctly. And it is our works of faith that prove whether or not we are handling them correctly (cf. James 2). It is because of this growth process that the writer states, "It is for discipline that you endure" (12:7).

## Words Are Important

The English words of these verses don't tell the full story. For example, take the word "discipline." We tend to think in terms of the rod, or a belt. But the Greek word *paideia* (discipline) means far more than that. It refers to the whole training and education of children. It involves the cultivation of mind and morals. It employs admonition, reproof, and punishment. In this context it is best understood as "God's training program."

The term "faint' (Gr. *ekluo*) means to become despondent or fainthearted, and the term "reproved" (Gr. *elegcho*) means to convict or point out a fault. Another important term is "scourge" (Gr. *mastigoo*) which means chastening and training by affliction. With these definitions in mind, lets develop a paraphrase of the text:

> *My son, do not take lightly the training program of the Lord, nor become despondent or fainthearted when He points out areas in your life that need work, for those whom the Lord loves He trains as*

*His children, and He chastens and trains by affliction every son whom He receives.*

Do you see the point? Everything that we face in life is a part of God's training program for us as His children. Nothing is excepted! And it is through this training program that we are matured and prepared to receive our inheritance. There is no other program. In its outworking, God affirms our faith as well as pointing out those areas that need work. The same circumstances can do both together. Further, God does not give up on us, He is faithful to the task.

Keep in mind, however, that the experience of it is not always pleasant. Nor is it intended to be. We may be called upon to face loneliness, sorrow, illness, pain, heartache, even death. We are reminded that "All discipline for the moment seems not to be joyful, but sorrowful" (12:11a). But if we hang in there with faith and obedience, and with the high expectation which faith brings, it will accomplish the objective: "yet to those who have been trained by it, afterwards it yields the peaceful fruit of righteousness" (12:11b).

# 5

# Look Out For The Enemy!

As if the growth process were not difficult enough by itself -- now we have to learn that someone is working overtime to keep us from the goal! Listen to this: "Be of sober spirit, be on the alert. Your adversary, the devil, prowls about like a roaring lion, seeking someone to devour" (I Pet. 5:8).

Sounds intimidating -- even frightening, doesn't it? Right now you might be asking yourself, "What chance do I really have of becoming fully mature or adequately prepared to receive my inheritance in Christ? I'm no match for Satan!" Yes and no. If you remain spiritually immature, you are right, you are no match for Satan. But on the other hand, if you cooperate with God's training program and live in faithful obedience to the

directives of His Word, then you have every reason to
expect to be victorious over the "roaring lion"!

In Ephesians 4:11-16, the Apostle Paul addresses the
process that God uses to equip us for growth. That
process is essentially this: evangelists and pastor/teachers,
through instruction and training, equip Believers for the
work of service, all with a view to the building up or
maturing of the Body of Christ.

Every Christian has an intended role in the process.
Using the metaphor of a human body, Christ is likened
to the head, while the individual Believers correspond to
its various joints and parts. It is described this way: "We
are to grow up in all aspects into Him, who is the head,
even Christ, from whom the whole body, being fitted and
held together by that which every joint supplies,
according to the proper working of each individual part,
causes the growth of the body for the building up of
itself in love" (vvs. 16,17). This maturity process will
continue until "we all attain. . .to a mature man, to the
measure of the stature which belongs to the fullness of
Christ" (vs. 13).

We can expect that if we are faithfully involved in the
process, we will be progressing toward becoming a fully
mature, productive adult. No longer will we remain
children. But what if we harden our hearts and the
Word becomes unprofitable in our lives -- like it did in
the case of the Hebrew Christians (Heb. 4)? What
happens if we remain children or regress back to being
children?

As a consequence of becoming spiritually mature, God's

Word says that we will "no longer be children" (vs. 14a).
But if we do not become mature, we will remain
children. And Paul describes what children are like: they
are "tossed here and there by waves, and carried about
by every wind of doctrine, by the trickery of men, by
craftiness in deceitful scheming" (vs. 14b). Quite a
picture! Children are unstable and easily led astray.
The term "craftiness" is particularly instructive. It is the
Greek word *kubeia*, which is used only once in the entire
New Testament. It has to do with "throwing dice."
Perhaps we can understand its intended meaning if we
paraphrase:

> *As a result of our becoming mature Christians we
> will no longer be children. Children are like a ship
> caught in a storm at sea, which is tossed here and
> there by waves -- by every new idea and teaching
> that comes along! They don't understand that they
> are being tricked and led astray from the truth. To
> put it bluntly, Christians who are uncooperative in
> God's training program, and thus remain children,
> are like those who would "shoot craps" with the
> devil -- and he has "loaded dice" -- there is no way
> they can win against him!*

The conflict between Satan (we'll use his title to refer to
the devil and his demons), and the Believer is commonly
referred to as "spiritual warfare." What is spiritual
warfare all about? How can we be victorious, not led
astray so as to remain immature and ultimately forfeit
our inheritance in Christ? Let's take a look.

## What Spiritual Conflict Is All About

There are two kingdoms currently functioning on earth: The Kingdom of Darkness and The Kingdom of Light - - the latter called in Colossians 1:13, "the kingdom of His beloved Son."

The Kingdom of Darkness is made up of spirit beings who are called variously in the Scriptures by the terms: evil spirits, demons, devils, principalities, powers, rulers of darkness, et al), and all unsaved humans. Satan rules as king over the Kingdom of Darkness.

The Kingdom of Light is made up of the righteous. That is, the unfallen angels and saved humans, with the Lord Jesus Christ reigning as King.

The Bible pictures these two kingdoms in conflict. Those in the Kingdom of Darkness (human beings) are said to be dead (spiritually) (Eph. 2:1). They do not possess eternal life (which involves both a relationship with God and a quality of existence). They are incapable of thinking God's thoughts -- having neither the desire or capacity to do so (Rom. 8:7; 1 Cor. 2:1-16). Because they reject God and have no desire to know or serve Him, they ascribe greater worth and value to the creation than to God (Rom. 1:25). Too, since they have not been freed from sin by faith in Christ, they are still enslaved to it. Consequently, they live to gratify their fleshly impulses and desires. They are totally self-serving (cf. Eph. 4:17-19).

The various philosophies of this world system (which is a manifestation of the Kingdom of Darkness), are nothing more than an articulation of its understanding of life and how it is to be lived. Being void of God's viewpoint, it represents man's best efforts to describe what has been, what is, and what shall be. Ultimately, the philosophies of this world system are attributable to Satan, who is said to be "the god of this world" (2 Cor. 4:4).

The warfare between the Kingdom of Darkness and the Kingdom of Light is said not to be "according to the flesh" (2 Cor. 10:3). It is spiritual warfare (Eph. 6:12). However, that is not to say that its outworking does not involve the issues of the flesh (physical), for the Scriptures make it certain that it does.

Whereas the Scriptures make it very clear that a Believer can not be possessed by Satan (there is not one biblical example of this ever happening), a Believer can be taken captive in the war. And because of Satanic brainwashing some will actually come under the control of Satan -- ultimately being used by him against the Kingdom of Light! (note Col. 2:8ff, and 2 Tim. 2:26).

Before we continue, let me state it emphatically that there is not one biblical example of a Believer ever being what is commonly called "demon possessed." There are examples of Believers being *influenced*, *controlled* (the term "filled" conveys the notion of "control and domination"), and *harassed* by satanic forces (Acts 5:3; 2 Cor. 12:7). Sometimes Believers are given over to Satan for discipline (cf. 1 Cor. 5:5), but even in that case there is no indication that they are ever "indwelt" or "possessed" by him. To put it another way, Satan's work against us is based from without, not from within.

## How Satan Operates

When it comes to spiritual warfare, the first thing that we need to understand is that we are totally responsible for our own choices. If we think, say or do something, it is because we have chosen to do so. Satan cannot force us to do anything against our will. Second, we need to realize that the battleground for spiritual warfare is the mind. Paul makes this very clear in 2 Cor. 10:3-5: "For though we walk in the flesh, we do not war according to the flesh, for the weapons of our warfare are not of the flesh, but divinely powerful for the destruction of fortresses. We are destroying speculations and every lofty thing raised up against the knowledge of God, and we are taking every thought captive to the obedience of Christ."

This is the most neglected area for most Christians. Although we are instructed to renew our minds on the Word of God (this being the way not to be conformed to this world system), most spend very little time in that process. How can we recognize error if we do not know the truth? How can we recognize and refute the empty philosophies of this world if we do not have a biblical world view? The most common result is being "tossed here and there by waves, and carried about by every wind of doctrine, by the trickery of men, by craftiness in deceitful scheming" (Eph. 4:14).

The methodology of Satan is deceit and fraud (cf. Rev. 12:9; 1 Tim. 4:1). In Acts 13:5-10, we have a record of Paul's encounter with a man representing the kingdom of darkness. Paul was reasoning with the proconsul at Salamis, Sergius Paulus, who is said to be "a man of intelligence" (vs. 7). However, a man called Elymus "was opposing them, seeking to turn the proconsul away from the faith" (vs. 8). Paul's rebuke of Elymus provides clear insight into how Satan operates in the war. "Paul, filled with the Holy Spirit, fixed his gaze upon him, and said, 'You who are full of all **deceit** and **fraud**, you son of the devil, you enemy of all righteousness, **will you not cease to make crooked the straight ways of the Lord?**'" (vvs. 9-10, emphasis mine). What Paul was involved in with Elymus is exactly what he stated in 2 Cor. 10:3-5.

Satan, through deceit and fraud attacks the Word of God with the goal of getting those in the Kingdom of Light to rebel against their King. If and to whatever extent he is successful, he actually gets those in the Kingdom of Light to obey him. In that sense they are under his control. Do not miss the main point: the battle is waged in the mind. If we do not have a clear biblical world view, we are vulnerable to deception and fraud. We will readily then buy into Satan's world view, for it will sound right (make sense)! It may even be -- and often is -- presented as biblical doctrine!

But not only is our weakened mind a problem, but our flesh is weak also. This is an additional area of vulnerability. When we become believers in the Lord Jesus Christ, we receive forgiveness for all our sins. We are declared "not guilty" by God because Christ died for our sins. Romans 6 informs us that whereas we were previously enslaved to sin, now, in Christ, we have been set free from its power in our lives. In other words, we are now free <u>not</u> to obey the lusts of our flesh. But we can still do so <u>if we choose</u> to! That is why the appeal of Scripture is to my mind and volition -- "Even so **consider** yourselves to be dead to sin, but alive to God in Christ.  Therefore **do not let** sin reign in your mortal body that you should obey its lusts,  and **do not go on presenting** the members of your body to sin as instruments of unrighteousness; but **present** yourselves to God as those alive from the dead, and your members as instruments of righteousness to God" (Rom. 6:11-13, emphasis mine).

We still have a problem with sin.  Our flesh is still with us.  We are no longer enslaved to it, but we have the continuing capacity to satisfy its lusts -- if we choose to!  The strategy of Satan is to try to get us who are now in the Kingdom of Light to rebel against God and His Word, and to gratify the lusts of our flesh.

## Areas Subject To Attack

1 John 2:16 lists three areas in which Satan mounts his attack, "For all that is in the world, **the lust of the flesh** and **the lust of the eyes** and **the boastful pride of life**, is not from the Father, but is from the world" (emphasis mine).  These are the things that are important to those in the Kingdom of Darkness.  They are captive to the lusts of the flesh.  They are driven by materialistic desires.  They want to be someone!  Their philosophy of life is totally (to borrow a word from their own system) narcissistic -- having an excessive admiration of oneself.

Satan approached our Lord in this same way.  In our day Satan uses the people in his kingdom (they are enslaved to their adamic nature and to the philosophies of this world), and especially its media to appeal to our capacity to leave God out. He makes it sound so good. We can be happy, fulfilled, powerful, rich -- and feel really good, if we will just do things his way. Perhaps a diagram of our Lord's temptation will help. The particulars are recorded in Matthew 4:1-11.

| AREA | APPEAL | RESPONSE |
|---|---|---|
| Lust of the flesh. | Physical needs. "Turn stones to bread." | "It is written." |
| Lust of the eyes. | Wealth. "Kingdoms of the world." | "It is written." |
| Sinful pride of life. | Accomplishments/Power/Etc. "Cast yourself down." | "It is written." |

Satan operates the same way with us. And we are to respond the same way that Jesus responded, on the basis of the Word of God. One additional comment with regard to the lust of the flesh, lust of the eyes, and the sinful pride of life. Because our flesh craves satisfaction, we have natural bends and desires in that direction. Those of the Kingdom of Darkness can only make their appeal to these areas. We are the ones who choose to satisfy them in inappropriate ways. We are totally responsible! No one in the Kingdom of Light is justified in making the claim, "The devil made me do it!"

## Some Concluding Thoughts

Satan and those of his kingdom will try to influence us by presenting arguments that are deceptive and untrue. They will try to convince us that we need certain things. That we must dress a certain way, smell a certain way, look a certain way, talk a certain way, believe a certain

way, behave a certain way, drive certain cars, live in
certain neighborhoods, have relationships with certain
people, etc. (the list is endless), if we are going to fit in,
be someone, and experience a full and meaningful life.

We can not be dominated or controlled by Satanic
seductions, or by the flesh, or the pride of life apart
from our own choices, but I am not sure that the
average Christian has the discernment to tell whether he
is a victor or a victim in the conflict. However, the
Word of God does provide us with a strategy for victory.
We are to be "taking every thought captive to the
obedience of Christ." This is what makes it possible for
us to be successful in "destroying speculations and every
lofty thing raised up against the knowledge of God" (2
Cor. 10:5). We are also to "take up the full armor of
God, that you may be able to resist in the evil day, and
having done everything, to stand firm" (Eph. 6:13). We
are further told to "Resist the devil and he will flee from
you" (James 4:7). Preeminent is the command found in
the first part of James 4:7 -- the real key to victory:
"Therefore submit to God."

Life is serious business. We have nothing to fear as long
as we walk with Christ. We cannot be victorious over
the world, the flesh or the devil by living in the strength
of our flesh. It is only as we continue to renew our
minds through God's Word and walk in the power of His
Spirit so as to experience victory and enjoy the eternal
life that is ours in Christ.

# 6

# Qualified to Inherit

The preacher was nearly in tears as he described the plight of a young boy who had become orphaned at age twelve and had lived on the streets for the next two years. His parents had been killed in a automobile accident and there were no relatives to care for him. Initially, he had been placed in a foster home, but in anger over the loss of his parents, he had run away.

Living on the street had been difficult -- particularly as a child. Adults could defend themselves and the police left them alone. But for a young boy it was a different story. He was constantly on the lookout for troublemakers and often he had to play "hide and seek" with the police.

Meals consisted mostly of what he would glean from the trash cans of nearby restaurants.

It was on a real cool evening in October, that he decided to sleep under a pile of cardboard boxes that had been discarded in the alley next to his "favorite restaurant." He hadn't been asleep long when he was awakened by the sound of a car door slamming and several voices.

"I wonder how he got here?" he heard one of them say. "Looks like a run-a-way to me," came the reply. Suddenly, he felt a big hand on his shoulder. "Wake up, son," the voice said. In an instant his eyes were as large as silver dollars. As he drew himself to his feet, there, before him, were three men -- one of whom was very well dressed, and obviously in charge of the other two.

"Why are you out here in the cold?" the well-dressed man asked. "Don't you have a home?" He could tell they were not the police. But who were they? "What do ya want to know for?" he shot back. "As we were driving past the alley I noticed you laying among those boxes and I was concerned that you might be hurt."

"No one cares about me," the boy said. "That's not true, I care," said the man. "Are you going to call the police?" asked the boy. "Have you done something wrong?" came the reply. "No!" exclaimed the boy. "Then come on and get into the car. I'll take you to my home. You can get something to eat and then get some rest.

Somewhat reluctantly he climbed into the car. Within a few minutes the car turned into an entrance that was flanked by big iron gates. A guard house soon appeared as they made their way down a long winding driveway.

"I've never seen such a house" the boy thought to himself as they pulled up in front of the house. The inside of the house was even more breathtaking. There were many large rooms, and a huge winding stairway leading to the second floor. "He must be a very rich man; I wonder who he is?"

By this time the preacher had everyone's attention. He went on to explain how the man built a relationship with the boy and actually adopted him as his own son and made him his heir. That, the preacher continued to explain is exactly what God did for us -- He adopted us into His family and we are now his children.

An interesting, emotionally charged story, but his application was totally inaccurate!

Ephesians 1:5 says that God "predestined us to the adoption as sons through Jesus Christ to Himself, according to the kind intention of His will." And like the preacher in our story, many have wrongly taught or have been taught that as a result of believing in Christ, one becomes a member of God's family by adoption.

We become a child of God by birth, not by adoption. The notion of "adoption as sons" is vitally important, but we must be careful to distinguish it from "being born again."

## Born of God

Unlike the young boy in the story, the condition of the unbeliever, the natural man is much worse. He is, in fact, dead! The Apostle Paul explains his condition like this: "And you were dead in your trespasses and sins, in which you formerly walked according to the course of this world, according to the prince of the power of the air, of the spirit that is now working in the sons of disobedience. Among them we too all formerly lived in the lusts of our flesh, indulging the desires of the flesh and of the mind, and were by nature children of wrath, even as the rest" (Eph. 2:1-3).

In that condition there are "none who seek for God" (Rom. 3:11); their mind is "hostile toward God; for it does not subject itself to the law of God, for it is not even able to do so" (Rom. 8:7).

Keep in mind that the natural man has the ability to believe or trust. This is human volition. It is an attribute of man. In fact, all people really live "by faith." Whatever one follows as a philosophy of life or world view becomes the basis of one's thoughts and actions. Therefore, life is lived on the basis of what one actually believes in or trusts.

The fundamental problem, however, is that the nature of the natural man is biased toward self and away from God. Being spiritually dead he "does not accept the things of the Spirit of God; for they are foolishness to him, and he cannot understand them, because they are spiritually appraised" (1 Cor. 2:14).

By nature, the natural man not only will not, but cannot believe in the gospel of Jesus Christ. Not having an ability to understand the wisdom of God, the gospel to him is "foolishness" (1 Cor. 1:18). That is why Jesus said "No one can come to Me, unless the Father who sent

Me draws him" (Jn. 6:44). However, He does add that "Everyone who has heard and learned from the Father, comes to Me" (Jn. 6:37). But who are those who hear and learn from the Father?

Jesus Himself identified them as "My sheep" (Jn. 10:1-30). He knows them and they know Him (vs. 14). He lays down His life for them (vs. 15). Those who are not His sheep do not believe in Him *because* they are not His sheep (vs. 26). Those who are His sheep will believe in Him (vs. 27); He gives eternal life to them (vs. 28a); and they shall never perish (vs. 28b).

Paul describes those who "hear and learn from the Father" as those chosen by God "before the foundation of the world" (Eph. 1:3); as those "foreknown" by God (Rom. 8:29); and as those uniquely formed by God as "vessels of mercy, which He prepared beforehand for glory" (Rom. 9:23).

It is true the natural man must believe in Christ to be saved (Acts 16:31). It is equally true that he cannot. The important question therefore is this: How, then, will anyone ever by saved?

The answer is, very simply, by the grace of God. One is not saved by faith, but by grace. Faith is the "pipe" through which it flows.

Because of man's lost condition, his salvation is totally the work of God [cf. 1 Cor. 1:30a; Eph. 2:5,8 ("have been saved" is in the Greek perfect tense -- completed action in past time with continuing results, and is in the passive voice); 1 Pet. 1:3], but the process does follow a logical order.

The whole process happens at the same moment, but because several things happen at that moment, a logical sequence is formed. 1 John 5:1 states that those who "believe that Jesus is the Christ (present tense) is (lit. has been) born of God (perfect tense). In grammatical sequence, the begetting precedes the believing.

It is amazing that a natural man can actually become born of God!  This is what Jesus explained to Nicodemus in John 3, "Unless one is born again, he cannot see the kingdom of God" (vs. 3).

Several clear examples of this process are presented in Scripture.  In 2 Thessalonians 2:13 Paul writes, "But we should always give thanks to God for you, brethren beloved by the Lord, because God has chosen you from the beginning for salvation through sanctification by the Spirit and faith in the truth.  And it was for this He called you through our gospel, that you may gain the glory of our Lord Jesus Christ."

In Acts 16:14 we are given the account of the first person to come to Christ in Europe.  "And a certain woman named Lydia, from the city of Thyatira, a seller of purple fabrics, a worshipper of God, was listening; and the Lord opened her understanding to respond to the things spoken by Paul."

The process seems clear enough:  those who have been chosen by the Father before the foundation of the world are those foreknown by Him, and they are those who are the sheep of the Lord Jesus Christ.  The Lord Jesus

Christ laid down His life for the sheep. He died in their place (cf. Matt. 20:28; Jn. 10:15; Rom. 5:8; 1 Pet. 1:17-18; et al). His death satisfied the justice of God for their sins (cf. Rom. 4:25). In a word, their salvation was totally and completely accomplished at the cross.

But the application of their salvation comes in time. Remember, we are speaking about logical sequence. At the point of regeneration by the Holy Spirit an individual is made alive. As a "new creation" (2 Cor. 5:17) this one, like the natural man, has the ability to believe or trust (thus making faith a gift of God's grace as well (cf. 2 Thess. 3:2; Phil. 1:29). Unlike his old nature that was biased away from God and toward self, his new nature is biased toward God. In this new created state the gospel is no longer "foolishness" to him -- it is now compelling (he is "called" through it (cf. 2 Thess. 2:14). He believes it, trusts it. And his act of believing becomes the evidence of his regeneration (cf. Jn. 6:29; 1 Cor. 12:3) -- it is his first work of faith. He is now a child of God -- by birth!

But, you may be asking yourself, what about all those passages that talk about being adopted? What is that all about?

## Adoption as Sons

Even with all its inaccuracies about how we become a part of God's family, our opening story does have an element of truth to it. We *have* "received the adoption as sons" (cf. Gal. 4:5). But as we have seen, "adoption" is not the way we became part of the family -- that is by birth. Adoption has to do with rights and privileges as an heir in the family. The term adoption is found only in the New Testament (Rom. 8:15, 23; 9:4; Gal. 4:5; Eph. 1:5), where it is developed into a theological concept -- and then only by Paul. There are two principle points to be made: 1. adoption stresses the release from slavery, where the former slave is granted all the rights and privileges as a son in the family; and 2. adoption is used to stress heirship -- that as a son, one is fully qualified to share in the inheritance of the father.

It is with the second principle that we are primarily concerned in this study. In Christ, God has fully qualified each of His children as an heir.

In Colossians 1:10-14, the apostle relates how a worthy walk with God manifests itself. Verse 12 states, "giving thanks to the Father, who has qualified us to share in the inheritance of the saints in light." The reason for this thankfulness is given in verse 13, "For He has delivered us from the domain of darkness, and transferred us to the kingdom of His beloved Son."

The phrase "who has qualified" is a translation of a Greek participle formed from the term *hikanoo*, which means "to make sufficient, to render fit." At the point of our regeneration -- when we were transferred from the kingdom of darkness into the kingdom of the Son, we were rendered fit by the Father as an heir.

## The Heir and The Inheritance

As we shall see in the next chapter, being qualified as an heir does not mean that every heir receives an equal share in the inheritance. The fact that an inheritance awaits us is well established. Peter tells us that our salvation from sin is with a view to "an inheritance which is imperishable and undefiled and will not fade away, reserved in heaven for you" (1 Pet. 1:4).

But there is also the matter of works of faith, a subject that we have fully developed in the ongoing chapters of this book. There is a direct relationship between our works of faith and our share in the inheritance in Christ.

To lay hold of all that is potentially ours in the inheritance we must flesh out the truth of God's Word in the momentary situations and circumstances of life. Paul had this in mind when he addressed the elders from Ephesus: "And now I commend you to God and the word of his grace, which is able to build you up and to give you the inheritance among all those who are sanctified" (Acts 20:32).

In his exhortation to the church at Colassae he said, "Whatever you do, do your work heartily, as for the Lord rather than for men; knowing that from the Lord you will receive the reward of the inheritance" (Col. 3:23-24).

Today, some of the things in our culture provide us with interesting illustrations. I remember well the wise counsel of a former theology professor. He would often remind his students not to push illustrations too far, for at some point they all break down. With that in mind, let's use a cultural situation to illustrate the relationship between salvation and inheritance.

Many professional athletes have what is termed a "no-cut contract with incentive clauses." Basically, it means that they have a secure position on the team -- they cannot be cut. As a member of the team, there are many things that he will share in common with the other players, simply because he is a member of the team. On the other hand, he has the opportunity to greatly increase his compensation through his performance. If he performs well, his compensation will be commensurate with his performance. If his performance is sub-standard, he will forfeit what could have been his.

The parallel is obvious. At the point of regeneration -- when we trust in Christ as our sin bearer, we are justified by God in a forensic sense whereby He declares us righteous and treats us as such. By His power we are kept in that state (cf. Jn. 10:27-30; 1 Pet. 1:5; 2 Tim. 2:13). As His children, we share many things in common, e.g. eternal life (Jn. 3:16); the righteousness of Christ (Rom. 3:22); a resurrection body (2 Cor. 15:50-58); the hope of heaven (Jn. 14:2,3; 2 Cor. 5:8); et al.

But there are things that are not shared in common -- specifically, rewards and inheritance. These actually become "incentive clauses." How well are you doing? In the next chapter we will look into the future to our final examination. Hopefully, it will spur us to action!

# 7

# Our Final Examination

The afternoon sun was very hot, but I hardly noticed. It was one of those rare moments of a lifetime. Sweat was rolling down my face and my heart was beating rapidly. I stood and watched as several dozen people walked ahead of me pointing out different things that caught their eye. It was an incredible experience. I was standing in the main area of the Corinthian Agora!

I had learned as a seminary student that every major city in ancient Greece had an agora (the Greek term for *marketplace*). It was very much like an open air shopping mall. This one was L-shaped with shops lining both sides of the walkway. Temples for Grecian gods were there. There was a meat market, too, where one could buy fresh meat that had been used in sacrifices to the Grecian gods. Even the tent-making shop of Aquila and his wife Priscilla was located there.

As I looked around, I tried to visualize the slave-trade that had been conducted there. Many human beings had been bought and sold in the Corinthian Agora! I also was well aware that it was here that Paul had had his day in court.

On his second missionary journey, Paul had been able to plant a Christian church in Corinth (Acts 18:1-17). In that day, Corinth was the metropolis of the Peloponnesus. It was strategically located on a narrow isthmus between the Aegean Sea and the Adriatic Sea that connects the Peloponnesus with northern Greece.

Corinth was a very religious city, being filled with shrines and temples -- the most prominent being the Temple of Aphrodite which was situated atop an 1,800-foot promontory called the Acrocorinthus. Worshipers took full advantage of the 1,500 Hieroduli (temple prostitutes) as they worshiped the "goddess of love."

The city thrived on commerce, entertainment, immorality and corruption, and was notorious as a place of wealth and indulgence. "To live as a Corinthian" meant to live in luxury and immorality. It was into this environment our Lord had sent Paul to plant His church.

When Paul came into a new city, it was his custom to go first to the Jewish synagogue, because it was there he could present Christ as Messiah and show how He had fulfilled the promises of the Law and Prophets. And in the process, God was pleased to save some of them.

But those of the Jews who did not believe reacted violently toward Paul. Acts 18 records how they took

Paul before Gallio, the proconsul of Achaia, charging that "This man persuades men to worship God contrary to the law" (vs. 13). Interestingly, the case was heard by Gallio at "the judgment seat" (vvs. 12, 16).

As I turned to look behind me, I noticed what appeared to be a stage or platform. It was about four to five feet high, and its floor area was about the size of the family room in our house in Texas. It was framed by a stone wall, and my eye immediately fixed on a Greek inscription carved into one of the stones: βημα (*bema*) -- the Greek term for "judgment seat." This was it, the judgment seat! The Corinthian church knew the *bema* well.

The Corinthian church has been characterized in this way: "Though gifted and growing, the church was plagued with problems: moral and ethical, doctrinal and practical, corporate and private." One of their problems was that they were taking each other to court over issues that should have been resolved in the church. Paul addresses the problem in 1 Cor. 6:1-8. But the point we are making is this: their litigation would have been addressed at the *bema* located in the *agora* at Corinth!

## A Picture Is Worth a Thousand Words

Modern research demonstrates that people have different styles of learning. Some are more analytical, others more conceptual, while still others require visualazition. Not that a person learns totally one way or the other, just that individuals tend to be dominated more by one particular style.

These observations are particularly helpful to those of us who are teachers. To help people learn, we must communicate not only with words, but also with "pictures" -- including verbal pictures.

Some 2,400 years ago, Solomon, King of Israel, said, "There is nothing new under the sun. Is there anything of which it may be said, 'See, this is new'?" (Eccl. 1:9).

God knew about the "wordless book" even before its value was discovered. He also knew pictures -- even verbal pictures, were a terrific aid to learning. He taught the Children of Israel through "pictures" (cf. 1 Cor. 10:3-4). Jesus used "verbal pictures" (parables) to teach His disciples (cf. Matt. 13:10-17).

The Apostle Paul also used "verbal pictures." True, he demonstrates a clear, logical style in his writing, for the most part conceptualizing truth. But he also makes good use of the culture and experiences of his audience to facilitate learning.

For example, the Christians in Corinth had observed, indeed many had taken part in, the buying and selling of slaves in the *agora*. To help them understand the doctrine of redemption and its attendant consequences, Paul selected the Greek term *agorazo*, which means *to purchase in the market place*. Here is how he put it, "Do you not know that your body is a temple of the Holy Spirit who is in you, whom you have from God, and that you are not your own? For you *have been bought* (*agorazo*) with a price: therefore glorify God in your body" (1 Cor. 6:19-20).

God had purchased them out of the "slave market" of sin, and they now belong to Him.

In his second letter to that same church, Paul carefully explained that the manner in which they conducted their lives was of critical significance. Everything you do, he said, should be done with the "ambition. . .to be pleasing to Him" (2 Cor. 5:9). But why? "For we must all appear before the judgment seat (*bema*) of Christ, that each one may be recompensed for his deeds in the body, according to what he has done, whether good or bad" (vs. 10).

Paul had said something about works and their value in his first letter (cf. 1 Cor. 3:10-15). But he hadn't used the term *bema*. Now they really have a clear picture of what it is all about. Someday every Believer will have to stand before the judge -- not Gallio, but the Lord Jesus Christ, and give an account of himself!

## The Judgment Seat of Christ

Standing in front of the *bema* in Corinth made a big impression on me. I could visualize myself standing in that public place and the Lord Jesus Christ standing in the seat of judgment. If I listened carefully, I could almost hear my name called.

"I wonder what I will receive," I thought to myself. I tried to run through the years of my life in a moment of time. The thousands upon thousands of thoughts that I had entertained in my mind, the words that I had spoken, the actions I had performed -- of what value were they, really?

Recall from earlier chapters that our soul-life is composed of our thoughts, words and actions. Recall, also, that the Scriptures state that these very components will be subjected to judgment (cf. 1 Cor. 4:5; Matt. 12:36; Eph. 6:8). Some of our thoughts, words and actions have been expressed on the basis of faith. These are what the Bible calls "good works" (Eph. 2:10), and "proof of faith" (1 Pet. 1:7). Everything else is referred to as "dead works" (Heb. 6:1; 9:14). Dead works, of course, are those that, before God, are useless and have no value.

At the judgment seat of Christ, the issue is not justification. That was accomplished at the cross and applied to every Believer in regeneration. The issue is rewards and inheritance. What rewards and inheritance are will be addressed in the next chapter. The subject of our current consideration is the relationship of rewards and inheritance to our soul-life and the judgment seat of Christ.

Paul says that each Believer will be "recompensed for his deeds." Earlier in this book we pointed out that the term recompense (Gr. *komizo*), means to receive back something that is due, or to get for one's self by earning.

Are we to understand that we actually earn something from God? Precisely! "But," someone will protest, "the Bible says that we are saved by grace through faith, and 'not as a result of works, that no one should boast'" (cf. Eph. 2:8-9). That is exactly our point. Although directly related to and growing out of justification, sanctification is distinct from it. The terms for sanctification are quite different from those of justification, and one makes an extremely serious error if that distinction is not acknowledged. If such acknowledgment is not made, the gospel of Christ becomes faith *plus* "works." Believe in Christ *plus* "Be baptized." Believe in Christ *plus* "Walk down the aisle." Believe in Christ *plus* "Make Him Lord of your life." The list is endless.

When a person trusts in Christ for the forgiveness of sins and eternal life, he is believing in One who *is* Lord! Whether or not he lives under the Lordship of Christ experientially is a different matter, as the example of the Corinthian church attests.

At the judgment seat of Christ, our works of faith actually earn rewards and inheritance. Remember the illustration of the professional athlete's no-cut contract with incentive clauses we discussed in the last chapter? When we are born of God -- regenerated - we become a "member of the team." At that point certain things become ours automatically: justification, the indwelling of the Holy Spirit, a new body, heaven, etc. But most aspects of the inheritance in Christ, including rewards, are the "incentive clauses."

"Incentive clause" accomplishments require commitment and choice. That is why we observe so many appeals to volition in the Scriptures. The imperative mood in New Testament Greek is used for this purpose. It is true that an imperative statement expresses a command. But the more fundamental intent of the imperative mood is to express appeal to volition. In fact, in New Testament Greek it is the strongest way to make an appeal to volition.

"Be diligent to present yourself approved to God as a workman who does not need to be ashamed, handling accurately the word of truth" (2 Tim. 2:15). "I, therefore, the prisoner of the Lord, entreat you to walk in a manner worthy of the calling with which you have been called" (Eph. 4:1). "Work out your salvation with fear and trembling" (Phil. 2:12). "Whatever you do, do your work heartily, as for the Lord rather than for men; knowing that from the Lord you will receive the reward of the inheritance. It is the Lord Christ whom you serve" (Col. 3:23-24). "You were called to freedom, brethren; only do not turn your freedom into an opportunity for the flesh, but through love serve one another" (Gal. 5:13).

These verses are examples of appeal to volition. To obey them expresses faith and commitment. Sometimes we obey, sometimes we don't. That's why at the judgment seat of Christ, judgment will be rendered "according to what he has done, whether good or bad" (2 Cor. 5:10).

## Tested By Fire

One can only imagine the scene in the agora's jewelry store -- people milling around the displays of gold, silver and precious stones. In the corner of the shop they could watch as ore was being placed in a large crucible and then heated until it reached a liquid state. When the ore reached that point, the dross -- the worthless part, was skimmed off, leaving the pure gold to be used for jewelry.

The process presented an interesting contrast. The fire

had an opposite effect on two of the elements involved: it burned up the wood used to heat the crucible, and it purified and made more valuable the precious metal contained in the crucible. No doubt Paul had observed this scene on many occasions. "Our works are just like that," he must have thought.

To make clear the relationship between works of faith, rewards, inheritance, and the judgment seat of Christ, he combined two aspects of the *agora:* the jewelry store and the judgment seat.

In 1 Corinthians 3:12-15 he sets it all out. Our works -- thoughts, words, actions, are likened to "gold, silver, precious stones, wood, hay, straw" (vs. 12). Obviously, the gold, silver and precious stones represent our *good works* (proof of faith). The wood, hay and straw represent our *dead works*.

In that day (the judgment seat of Christ), the quality of our work will become evident, "for it is to be revealed with fire" (vs. 13a). Our soul-life is the sum total of our works -- good works, dead works. The issue, therefore, is quality or value, and Paul adds "the fire itself will test the quality of each man's work" (vs. 13b).

Peter used this identical "picture" when he said, "the proof of your faith,. . .even though tested by fire, may be found to result in praise and glory and honor at the revelation of Jesus Christ" (1 Pet. 1:7).

For the term *test*, both writers chose the Greek word *dokimazo*. This is important. The judgment seat of Christ is not with a view to condemnation. That issue was settled at the cross. The fact is clearly stated in Romans 8:1, "There is therefore now no condemnation for those who are in Christ Jesus." And the New Covenant adds, "And their sins and their lawless deeds I will remember no more" (Heb. 10:17).

*Dokimazo* means to put something to the test, to examine something, with the thought of giving approval to it.

A young lady in our church once told me the story of how she had been walking in the local mall and noticed a sign in the window of a jewelry store that read, "Free Appraisals." She had recently been given a diamond engagement ring and wondered about its value. When she went into the store, the jeweler took the ring, put a glass magnifier in his eye and examined (*dokimazo*) the stone. The examination was not for the purpose of condemning the stone -- although the same examination could have certainly proven it to be of no value had that been the case. Fortunately for her the stone was proven to be valuable!

When our Lord evaluates our works, the fire of Paul's illustration represents the test. Perhaps this is what John the Baptist had in mind when he said, "As for me, I baptize you with water; but One is coming who is mightier than I, and I am not fit to untie the thong of His sandals; He will baptize you with the Holy Spirit and fire" (LK. 3:16). Jesus Christ baptizes us with the Holy Spirit at the beginning (the point of regeneration, cf. Acts 11:15-16), and baptizes us with fire at His judgment seat.

Well, here we are -- at the judgment seat of Christ. Our works are before us and the Savior has a torch in His hand. What will be the outcome? "If any man's work remains," Paul said, "he shall receive a reward" (vs. 14).

My own accumulation of works is soon hidden from view by the smoke as the "wood, hay and straw" is quickly consumed. It is quite a shock to watch, as it appears my life is literally "going up in smoke!"

Soon the smoke clears. The pile, certainly a lot smaller than it was, is, thank God, not a total loss!

I'm constrained to think what could have been mine if only I had chosen to more completely "lose my life for Christ's sake." Paul had warned me. "If any man's work is burned up, he shall suffer loss." It's obvious to me now that the loss he had in mind was all that might have been mine. My actual rewards are based on what is left, what has abiding value, what remains as proof of my faith -- the "gold, silver and precious stones."

Looking back on my life, it is all now so clear. My soul-life, represented by thoughts, words and actions, has actually been exchanged for a share in the rewards and inheritance I'm to receive in Christ. In that sense I have saved or delivered my soul-life into eternity. As Peter put it, "Obtaining as the outcome of your faith the salvation of your souls" (1 Pet. 1:9).

But what exactly are my rewards and inheritance? What is it that awaits me at the end of the "race of life?" To this subject we now turn our attention.

# 8

## Our Inheritance in Christ

**W**hat a magnificent thought! As believers in Christ we are the appointed heirs to the kingdom of God!

Like you, I have heard of people inheriting large fortunes, but that kind of thing is so foreign to my experience it is difficult to really grasp what it means. In all likelihood most people feel the same way. At best it can be little more than a dream.

The same thing is true when we talk about our being an heir of God. What does it mean? What will we inherit? Are there any conditions to be met? These are only a few of the many questions that might be asked. But as we come to the end of this book what better subject could we address than what will be ours -- or might have been ours -- in life everlasting.

## An Important Warning

In 1 Corinthians 6:9-10 and Ephesians 5:5, the Apostle Paul makes the strong assertion that certain people will not inherit the kingdom of God! Listen to what he says: "For this you know with certainty, that no immoral or impure person or covetous man, who is an idolater, has an inheritance in the kingdom of Christ and God" (Eph. 5:5). "Or do you not know that the unrighteous shall not inherit the Kingdom of God? Do not be deceived; neither fornicators, nor idolaters, nor adulterers, nor effeminate, nor homosexuals, nor thieves, nor covetous, nor drunkards, nor revilers, nor swindlers, shall inherit the kingdom of God" (1 Cor. 6:9-10).

Some have taken the phrase "kingdom of God" to refer to heaven and teach that if a person who claims to be a Christian commits any of these sins it means that he loses his salvation and will not go to heaven. Others say if a person who claims to be a Christian "practices" such sins it indicates that he was not really saved at all (recognizing that once a person is saved he cannot be lost again). But are these views supported by either context? The answer is a clear NO!

In 1 Corinthians 6, Paul is contrasting unbelievers with believers to exhort believers to godly living. In verse 11 he states, "And such were some of you; but you were washed, but you were sanctified, but you were justified in the name of the Lord Jesus Christ, and in the Spirit of our God." The Corinthians were living very much like unbelievers. In fact Paul asks them, "Are you not walking like mere men?" (1 Cor. 3:3). What did he have in mind? Just this: when they were saved they were characteristically fleshly because they were babes -- they didn't know any better; but now five years later they are still fleshly. Why? They had refused to grow! (cf. 1 Cor. 3:1-2). They had had very good teaching (Paul, Apollos, Peter), but they had not lived out what they had been taught. As a result they had not grown spiritually.

In chapter six he warns them about the consequences of living in the flesh -- which is opposite of living in the Spirit by faith. His argument essentially is this:  since unbelievers do not inherit the kingdom of God, why should you want to live like them?  To do so is totally unprofitable, and the implication is that you forfeit your inheritance in the kingdom to the extent you choose to live like them!

Clearly Paul is not saying they forfeit heaven -- regeneration took them from being *one of them* to being what they are, children of God. He is saying they forfeit some aspects of the inheritance that might have been theirs! The context of the Ephesians passage teaches the same thing.

From what we have developed in earlier chapters of this book and what we have just presented, I hope God has your attention.  If we do not live to please God -- living by faith within the parameters of His word, we forfeit our inheritance in Christ!  That really makes life a serious business, doesn't it!

## A Review of Some Basics

As believers in Christ we have been born into God's family (1 Jn. 5:1), and He has thereby qualified us as His heirs (Rom. 8:17; Col. 1:12). Thus the inheritance is established now and in the future will be realized (1 Pet. 1:4). Some aspects of the inheritance are shared by all believers: justification (Rom. 5:1), the unconditional righteousness of Christ (Rom. 3:22), reconciliation (Rom. 5:11), heaven (Jn. 14:2-3), a resurrection body (1 Cor. 15:50-58), et al.

However, some aspects of the inheritance are conditional. Listen to the Scripture: "And now I commend you to God and to the word of His grace, which is able to build you up and give you the inheritance among all those who are sanctified" (Acts 20:32).

Paul is saying these words to the elders of the church at Ephesus. The emphasis of the statement is on their relationship to God's word. Lived out in life it is able to do two things: 1. build them up in maturity; and 2. give them the inheritance in Christ. Clearly the reverse is true. If they do not live out God's word in life, they will not mature spiritually and will in the end forfeit the inheritance that could have been theirs!

Because most Christians don't like to think about "earning" anything from God, they react emotionally against any view of sanctification that speaks of works. But God tells us that we were "created in Christ Jesus for good works, which God prepared beforehand, that we should walk in them" (Eph. 2:10). And we should also understand that our works of faith actually earn inheritance: "Whatever you do, do your work heartily, as for the Lord rather than for men; knowing that from the Lord you will receive the reward of the inheritance. It is the Lord Christ whom you serve" (Col. 3:23-24).

## Gaining A Clear Perspective

As we think in terms of putting some definition to the various aspects of the inheritance, we need to be sure we have the big picture in mind. Let me explain.

When God created the first man, Adam, he gave him (and the human race that existed in Adam) a commission: mankind was to rule over the earth. The scope of that rule was stated in this way: "Let them rule over the fish of the sea and over the birds of the sky and over the cattle and over all the earth, and over every creeping thing that creeps on the earth" (Gen. 1:26). He was to "subdue it and rule [over it]" (Gen. 1:28). But because of Adam's sin, we do not see man ruling over the earth in this way. However, the thought of man one day ruling over the earth passed from generation to generation.

Having been in Israel and walked in the areas around Bethlehem where the shepherds tended their sheep, in my mind's eye I can picture David sitting on a hillside one evening looking up into the heavens. The sky is clear and the stars seem to number in the millions. The moon is shining brightly. He later records his thoughts of that moment: "When I consider Thy heavens, the work of Thy fingers, the moon and the stars, which Thou hast ordained; What is man, that Thou dost take thought of him? And the son of man, that Thou dost care for him? Yet Thou hast made him a little lower than God, and dost crown him with glory and majesty! Thou dost make him rule over the works of Thy hands; Thou hast put all things under his feet, all sheep and oxen, and also the beasts of the field, the birds of the heavens, and the fish of the sea, whatever passes through the paths of the sea. O Lord, our Lord, how majestic is Thy name in all the earth!" (Psm. 8:3-9).

David clearly understood the commission that God had given to mankind. But he didn't understand any more than Adam. He saw the rule of man as being over sheep and oxen, beasts of the field, birds of the heavens , and the fish of the sea. Is this it? Is there more? And when and how will it take place?

We must keep in mind the progressive nature of God's revelation. It would not be until the first century A.D. that God would supply the answers to these questions. We find them in part in the letter to the Hebrews. In the first chapter the writer tells us that God has appointed the Lord Jesus Christ "heir of all things" (v. 2). He has given Him the name "Son" in the sense of "first-born and heir." As such He will rule over all creation. Every creature will bow before Him. Paul put it this way: "God highly exalted Him, and bestowed on Him the name which is above every name, that at the name of Jesus every knee should bow, of those who are in heaven, and on earth, and under the earth, and that every tongue should confess that Jesus Christ is Lord, to the glory of God the Father" (Phil. 2:9-11).

The Lord Jesus Christ is the last Adam -- the Adam of Genesis being the first (1 Cor. 15:45). In the first Adam, all die. But in the last Adam, Christ, all shall be made alive (1 Cor. 15:22). In other words, there are two human races. One which is made up of every human being that is born into this world, and the other made up of human beings who have been born of the Spirit of God. Those of the second human race are referred to as the "sons of God" (Rom. 8:14), and the "many brethren" of the Lord Jesus Christ (Rom. 8:29). Jesus actually refers to those who believe in Him as "my brethren" (Heb. 2:11-12).

Now think about the commission to "man." Could it be that God had the second human race in mind the whole time? Let's take a look.

In Hebrews 2 the writer states that God "did not subject to angels the world to come" (v. 5). But notice the passage he quotes to state who will rule over the world to come: "What is man, that Thou rememberest him? Or the son of man, that Thou art concerned about him? Thou hast made him for a little while lower than the angels; Thou hast crowned him with glory and honor, and hast appointed him over the works of thy hands; Thou hast put all things in subjection under his feet" (vv. 6-8).

It is interesting that the writer stops short of the application that David saw -- animals, birds and fish. He ends with "Thou hast put *all things* in subjection under his feet" (emphasis mine). Now look at his application: "For in subjecting all things to him, He left nothing that is not subject to Him. But we do not yet see all things subjected to him. But we do see Him who was made for a little while lower than the angels, namely, Jesus, because of the suffering of death crowned with glory and honor" (vv. 8-9).

The commission to "man" finds its fulfillment in the Lord Jesus Christ! He is Heir of all things! The inheritance of God is for the Son and his many brethren. But there is a subtle aspect to this that is seldom pointed out, and we need to consider it carefully.

In God's sovereign plan for the ages, He has decreed everything that will ever come to pass. However, it is important also to remember that not only has He decreed the ends of all things, but also the *means* to those ends. Let's apply this principle to the issue at hand.

In eternity past God decreed that man (the human race) would ultimately rule over His creation. And the human race He had in mind was the second human race headed by the Lord Jesus Christ. But how could this be done? Through the incarnation!

John 1 tells us that the Word, Who was with God and was God, "became flesh, and dwelt among us, and we beheld His glory, glory as of the only begotten from the Father, full of grace and truth" (vv. 1, 14). Being born of a woman, He gained His humanity, thus becoming the God-Man -- fully God and fully man united in one person forever.

Anticipating His ultimate fulfillment of the commission given to "man" Christ Jesus mostly referred to Himself as "Son of Man" (cf. Matt. 8:20; 9:6; 10:23; 11:19; 12:8, 32, 40; 13:37, 41; et al).

In this book we have argued that our inheritance in Christ is based on works of faith. If you are still wrestling with the concept, I trust that what follows will dispel all doubt.

Remember the principle of "means to the end"? Consider this: our Lord gained *His* inheritance through His obedience to the Father! Thus He becomes an example for us!

Listen to His prayer in John 17: "Father, the hour has come; glorify Thy Son, that the Son may glorify Thee, even as Thou gavest Him authority over all mankind, that to all whom Thou hast given Him, He may give eternal life. And this is eternal life, that they may know Thee the only true God, and Jesus Christ whom Thou hast sent. I glorified Thee on the earth, having accomplished the work which Thou hast given Me to do. And now, glorify Thou Me together with Thyself, Father, with the glory which I ever had with Thee before the world was" (vv. 1-5).

Now put this together with what Paul writes in Philippians 2: "Have this attitude in yourselves which was also in Christ Jesus, who, although He existed in the form of God, did not regard equality with God a thing to be grasped, but emptied Himself, taking the form of a bond-servant, and being made in the likeness of men. And being found in appearance as a man, He humbled Himself by becoming obedient to the point of death, even death on a cross. Therefore, God also highly exalted Him, and bestowed on Him the name which is above every name, . . ."(vv. 5-9).

Don't miss the point: the exaltation of the Son came as a consequence of His obedience! And as the First-born of the second human race, it is *His* inheritance that we share!

One final point before we move on. In Romans 8 Paul addresses the subject of our being "children of God" (v. 16). As children of God we are qualified as heirs -- having received the "adoption as sons" (v. 15). Consequently, we are *all* "heirs of God" (v. 17). This refers to the portion of the inheritance we share in common because we are "children of God." But the First-born is a double-portion heir (an historically established fact). To share in the blessings of the First-born requires commitment and obedience. Listen to what Paul says: "If children, heirs also, heirs of God and fellow-heirs with Christ, if indeed we suffer with Him in order that we may be glorified with Him" (v. 17). In other words, if we are going to share in Christ's inheritance, we must enter into His sufferings through obedient, faithful living in the light of God's word.

**The Inheritance of Christ**

Since we know that *our* inheritance is related to *Christ's* inheritance, let's look at His first.

Our Lord's rule is over all creation, i.e. "all things" (Heb. 2:8). Some of it is expressed temporally -- as Israel's King. His rule is "over the house of Jacob" (Lk. 1:33); and "over the gentiles" (Rom. 15:12).

The temporal expression of the kingdom will be for "a thousand years" (Rev. 20:6); and He will reign "until He has put all His enemies under His feet" (1 Cor. 15:25). Moving on from the temporal, His kingdom is said to be "forever and ever" (Rev. 11:15).

The Old Testament tells us a great deal about the temporal expression of the kingdom. It is related primarily to the literal promises to Abraham and his seed. Yet we know very little about the eternal kingdom.

## The Inheritance of Believers

One of the problems we face in dealing with our inheritance is that the Scriptures use very general terms to describe it. Even so, we can gain enough insight to be able to build a fairly clear picture of what it will be like. Some of the terms address the inheritance directly, while others, like crowns and the promises to the overcomers in Revelation 2 and 3, seem to particularize the inheritance for certain individuals. The more general expressions include:

*The earth.* "Blessed are the gentle, for they shall inherit the earth" (Matt. 5:5).

*Eternal life.* "And everyone who has left houses or brothers or sisters or father or mother or children or farms for My name's sake, shall receive many times as much, and shall inherit eternal life" (Matt. 19:29; cf. Mk. 10:17; Lk. 10:25; 18:18).

*The kingdom.* "Then the King will say to those on His right, 'Come, you who are blessed of My Father, inherit the kingdom prepared for you from the foundation of the world'" (Matt. 25:34).

*An Imperishable Body.* "Now I say this, brethren, that flesh and blood cannot inherit the kingdom of God; nor does the perishable inherit the imperishable" (1 Cor. 15:50).

*Salvation.* "Are [angels] not all ministering spirits, sent out to render service for the sake of those who will inherit salvation?" (Heb. 1:14).

*The promises.* "And we desire that each one of you show the same diligence so as to realize the full assurance of hope until the end, that you may not be sluggish, but imitators of those who through faith and patience inherit the promises" (Heb. 6:11-12).

*A blessing.* "To sum up, let all be harmonious, sympathetic, brotherly, kind-hearted, and humble in spirit; not returning evil for evil, or insult for insult, but giving a blessing instead; for you were called for the very purpose that you might inherit a blessing" (1 Pet. 3:8-9).

When we look at the matter of *rewards*, the first thing we learn is that they will be received in heaven: "Blessed are you when men revile you, and persecute you, and say all kinds of evil against you falsely, on account of Me. Rejoice, and be glad, for your reward in heaven is great" (Matt. 5:11-12; cf. Matt. 16:12; Rev. 22:12).

The second thing we learn is that rewards are related to an obedient faith (good works/proof of faith):

"For if you love those who love you, what reward have you? Do not even the tax-gatherers do the same?" (Matt. 5:46).

"For the Son of Man is going to come in the glory of His Father with His angels; and will then recompense every man according to his deeds" (Matt. 16:27).

"Now he who plants and he who waters are one; but each will receive his own reward according to his own labor" (1 Cor. 3:8).

"If any man's work. . .remains, he shall receive a reward" (1 Cor. 3:14).

"Let no one keep defrauding you of your prize" (Col. 2:18).

"Watch yourselves, that you might not lose what we have accomplished, but that you may receive a full reward" (2 Jn. 8).

The matter of *crowns* gets a lot more personal. A crown is a *symbol* of victory, honor, or distinction. Therefore, to crown someone is to confer upon them honor, dignity, or reward.

We need to realize that what we learned as unbelievers, and what Satan tries to get us to do now, is to seek the honor of men. It is a part of this world system. People will do unbelievable things for a plaque to go on their wall, a trophy to put on their mantle, etc. Did not the Lord warn us about this kind of motivation: "Beware of practicing your righteousness before men to be noticed by them; otherwise you have no reward with your Father who is in heaven. When therefore you give alms, do not sound a trumpet before you, as the hypocrites do in the synagogues and in the streets, that they may be honored by men. Truly I say to you, they have their reward in full" (Matt. 6:1-2).

We need to think in eternal terms, not in temporal. That which is temporal will perish. Paul put it this way: "Do you not know that those who run in a race all run, but only one receives the prize? Run in such a way that you may win. And everyone who competes in the games exercises self-control in all things. They then do it to receive a perishable wreath, but we an imperishable" (1 Cor. 9:24-25).

Crowns can also be forfeited: "I am coming quickly; hold fast what you have, in order that no one take your crown" (Rev. 3:11).

There are four crowns that are mentioned:

(1) *Crown of righteousness.* "I have fought the good fight, I have finished the course, I have kept the faith; in the future there is laid up for me the crown of righteousness, which the Lord, the righteous judge, will award to me on that day; and not only to me, but to all who have loved His appearing" (2 Tim. 4:7-8).

(2) *Crown of glory and honor.* "Thou hast crowned him [man] with glory and honor" (Heb. 2:7; cf. 2:9).

(3) *Crown of life.* "Blessed is the man who perseveres under trial; for once he has been approved, he will receive the crown of life, which the Lord has promised to those who love Him" (Ja. 1:12; cf. Rev. 2:10).

(4) *Crown of glory.* "I exhort the elders among you, as

your fellow-elder and witness of the sufferings of Christ, and partaker also of the glory that is to be revealed, shepherd the flock of God among you, not under compulsion, but voluntarily, according to the will of God; and not for sordid gain, but with eagerness; not yet as lording it over those allotted to your charge, but proving to be examples to the flock. And when the Chief Shepherd appears, you will receive the unfading crown of glory" (1 Pet. 5:1-4).

The final aspect regarding our inheritance has to do with the promises to the overcomers. In 1 John 5:3-5, we are told that the love of God is to "keep His commandments" (v. 3a); and then John adds that "His commandments are not burdensome" (v. 3b). Our love for God manifests itself in obedience to His word (cf. Jn. 14:14, 21, 23-24). When we live in obedience to His word we are overcoming the world, the flesh and the devil; the lust of the eyes, the lust of the flesh, and the sinful pride of life (cf. Rom. 12:2; Gal. 5:16-17; Ja. 4:7; 1 Jn. 2:15-17).

For the sum of these John uses the term "world", and he anticipates that all believers will to some extent be overcomers (v. 4a). Indeed, because of faith in Christ as our Savior we have "overcome," and are the only ones who can keep on overcoming: "And who is the one who overcomes the world, but he who believes that Jesus is the Son of God?" (v. 5).

When John came to write the Book of Revelation, the Lord Jesus Christ gave him promises to communicate to those who were to overcome. Relating this to our earlier study, all believers are overcomers in the sense of being saved from the penalty of sin. However, not all believers continue on to become overcomers!

To borrow an earlier illustration, when the nation of Israel left Egypt it pictured our redemption in Christ. Their looking to their inheritance which God had set before them pictures our looking to our inheritance in Christ that is reserved in heaven for us. In essence, God told them, "Your inheritance (the land) is set before you -- it is yours, but you must possess it. You must overcome what is in the land. Do not inter-marry with the people in the land, do not make agreements with them -- drive them out of the land and possess it. I have given you all the resources you need, and I will fight your battles for you."

Ironically, they never totally possessed the land. Why? Because of disobedience and unbelief. They forfeited what could have been theirs! And we can do the same thing. We forfeit aspects of our promised inheritance if we fail to be overcomers.

Let's look at the promises to the overcomers. Since there are some promises to all believers, we list these first.

*"To him who overcomes, I will grant to eat of the tree of life which is in the Paradise of God"* (Rev. 2:7). What Adam lost we gain in Christ: "This is the bread which came down from heaven; not as the fathers ate, and died, he who eats this bread shall live forever" (Jn. 6:58).

*"He who overcomes shall not be hurt by the second death"* (Rev. 2"11). Jesus said, "Whoever lives and believes in

Me shall never die" (Jn. 11:26).

*"He who overcomes shall thus be clothed in white garments; and I will not erase his name from the book of life"* (Rev. 3:5a).    Romans 3:22 says that our righteousness is a righteousness "by faith in Jesus Christ." The theme of white garments is used in two ways: (1) to refer to our positional righteousness (Rev. 7:14); and (2) to our works of righteousness (Rev. 19:8). The second half of the statement is an affirmation of what our Lord said in John 10:27-28, "My sheep hear My voice, and I know them, and they follow Me; and I give eternal life to them, and they shall never perish; and no one shall snatch them out of my hand."

*"He who overcomes,...I will write upon him the name of My God and the name of the city of My God, the new Jerusalem, which comes down out of heaven from My God. And I will write on him My new name"* (Rev. 3:12b). This promise stresses our identification with God. Every believer is both *with* God and *identified* with God.

As we said earlier, there are also conditional promises given to those who are overcomers in a continuing sense. These are the promises not shared in common.

*"To him who overcomes, to him I will give some of the hidden manna, and I will give him a white stone, and a new name written on the stone which no one knows but he who receives it"* (Rev. 2:17). This promise stresses the fact that there will be different levels of relationship with the Lord in heaven. Like John 14:21, it stresses intimacy and familiarity: "He who has My commandments and keeps them, he it is who loves Me; and he who loves Me

shall be loved by My Father, and I will love him, and will disclose Myself to him."

*"He who overcomes. . .I will confess his name before My Father, and before His angels"* (Rev. 3:5b). In the context of Matthew 11, our Lord is teaching His disciples about persecution and their active identification with Him. In verses 32 and 32 He said, "Every one there who shall confess Me before men, I will also confess him before My Father who is in heaven. But whoever shall deny Me before men, I will also deny him before My Father who is in heaven." He ends the discourse by relating it to the possible loss of rewards (vv. 40-42).

*"He who overcomes, and he who keeps My deeds until the end, to him I will give authority over the nations; and he shall rule them with a rod of iron, as the vessels of the potter are broken to pieces, as I also have authority from My Father; and I will give him the morning star"* (Rev. 2:26-28). Another promise puts it much the same way: *"He who overcomes, I will grant him to sit down with Me on My throne, as I also overcame and sat down with My Father on His Throne"* (Rev. 3:21). Those who overcome will reign with Christ in power and authority. This is not for every believer. Paul wrote to Timothy that "If we endure, we shall also reign with Him" (2 Tim. 2:12a).

*"He who overcomes, I will make him a pillar in the temple of My God, and he will not go out from it any more"* (Rev. 3:12a). This has to do with priestly privilege and growth (cf. Zech. 3:1-10).

Although this chapter has been longer than the others, we certainly have not exhausted all that could be said about our inheritance. It is a vitally important subject, yet one sadly neglected. As we approach the coming of our Savior, the Spirit of God is moving to make these truths more widely known -- and you can help! Spread the word. Share this book with your friends and loved ones. The time to spread the greatness of this message is now!

Remember the words of our Lord Jesus Christ -- His last words recorded by John in the Book of Revelation:

> "Behold, I am coming quickly, and My reward is with Me, to render to every man according to what he has done" (Rev. 22:12).

This book is available from:

**Scriptel Publishers**
P. O. Box 691046
Houston, Texas 77269-1046
(713) 893-8412